Basic
Principles
of
Effective
Teaching

by June Crabtree

STANDARD PUBLISHING

Cincinnati, Ohio   3653

illustrations by Steve Hayes

Library of Congress Cataloging in Publication Data

Crabtree, June.
  Basic principles of effective teaching.

  1. Christian education.   2. Christian education—
Teaching methods.   I. Title.
BV1471.2.C72   268'.6   81-16585
ISBN 0-87239-454-9   AACR2

Foreword

What is good teaching? This question often puzzles the beginning teacher, and sometimes the experienced teacher. Educational terminology can be confusing when we try to determine the answer to this question. Is the good teacher one who is "modern," or "individualizing," or one who uses small groups, or engages in team teaching? The truth is that good teaching can be any of these things.

Good teaching has always been the same. When the learner learns, and wants to learn more, good teaching has taken place. Why? Certain basic elements are always found in good teaching. Really good teachers do the same kinds of things. That is what this book is all about.

If you want to be a good teacher, read about and try the methods used by good teachers everywhere. You will not find every technique in this book, but you will find the basic elements of good teaching. If you use them, you will be practicing basic methods of good teaching. As you grow in experience, you can develop similar, new methods of your own and become a truly creative teacher.

The first step you must take, if you are to become a good teacher, is to fully recognize and accept the fact that God has made each child and each adult different. Every ten-year-old is **not the same!** The adults in your classes have many differences! It has been for our convenience in organization that we have put all ten-year-olds and all young married adults in classes together.

The same God has given gifts to all of us—but He, in His great wisdom, did not give us all the same gifts! The apostle Paul told the Corinthians:

"Now there are diversities of gifts, but the same Spirit.
And there are differences of administrations, but the same Lord.
And there are diversities of operations, but it is the same God
which worketh all in all." (1 Corinthians 12:4-6)

Paul recognized diversities in matters dealing with people, because he knew God created each man and woman with unique skills and talents. You are reading this book because you have been given the gift of teaching. As you work to develop your gift, keep in mind that each student you teach will have different and unique gifts. Each student will have different strengths and abilities. As a good teacher, you will need to be aware of them. You may think it is an impossible task—to teach each one differently. Teaching is hard work if it is properly done. But I am convinced that there is no more rewarding "gift" from God than the gift of teaching.

Are basic teaching skills and individualizing incompatible? Not at all. Even though some have confused efforts to meet the needs of individual students, or "individualizing," with some of the undesirable aspects of modern innovations in public schools, recognizing individual differences is as old as the Bible itself.

You can meet individual needs. How, you ask? Obviously, there is more than one way. You will find some basic suggestions in this book. To these ideas, you will add your own ideas for your own individual pupils. You will select what you think will work for you.

After that, you will revise and perfect your ideas. Then you will be following your commission to use *your gift*—you will be using the *principles basic for effective teaching,* and you will be individualizing your teaching!

Keep in mind that, without realizing it, you are already using many of the techniques of good teaching. The purpose of this book is to help you see the best of your teaching in a new light and learn how to do more of the same. Hopefully, you will find some new ideas to help you increase the learning of each child in your class.

Effective instruction includes the use of many techniques. It can take place with a large group, or a small group. It does not necessitate one teacher and one child to achieve the maximum amount of learning. It is not one technique or organizational pattern, but the use of many different teaching styles and systems. It can be team teaching, discussing, reporting, or demonstrating. It can be working alone, with a partner, in a small group, or in a large group. If your students are learning, and wanting to learn more, then you *must* be using good methods and meeting individual needs.

It is important to remember that children will bring to each new learning experience their own information or misinformation. The teacher must seek ways to bring these varied backgrounds into the classroom in order for learning to be effective. To do this we must find different ways to use time and materials, or differentiate our instruction. Grouping patterns may need to be different. Schedules and use of classroom space may change.

In years past, if a child did not learn, the tendency was to use one of these phrases:

"He is lazy."

"She doesn't care."

"She has poor work habits."

"He has home problems."

"He has emotional problems."

"Her parents are separated."

"She is a slow learner."

and on and on. You have heard them all, and probably others. If you are honest, you may have to admit that you, too, have used some of these "reasons" for poor work. We must realize, however, that the teacher's responsibility is not simply to transmit information, then dodge behind one of these pat reasons if a child doesn't learn. *The teacher's responsibility continues until the child has learned.*

Teachers must seek out new and different materials to motivate students to learn. The same lesson may need to be taught at various levels of difficulty to suit each child's ability and background.

Diagnose is a key word in public school instruction, and it should be the Bible school teacher's most valuable technique. Diagnose means to *get to know all you can about the child.* Take time to really listen when students talk to you. Call in their homes. Learn their interests. Can each student read one paragraph in your lesson paper without making more than five errors? (If not, the material is too difficult for them to read alone.) Become acutely aware of each student as an individual, and you will realize that the many personality differences in your class will demand varied approaches to learning. *Learning will never be improved by ignoring the differences in your class. It cannot be repeated enough that this basic, underlying principle is essential for effective teaching.*

Remember that the student who has learned is the student who is able to do something he or she was not able to do before your teaching took place! A change has taken place in the student as the result of your teaching.

Before this change can take place in students, a change may need to take place in the attitude of the teacher. If you are ready to explore, to be creative, to try some new ideas, then this book is for you! Basic principles are effective and exciting. Try them!

June Crabtree

"We have different gifts, according to the grace given us. If a man's gift is . . . teaching, let him teach; if it is encouraging, let him encourage; if it is contributing to the needs of others, let him give generously . . ."
(Romans 12:6-8, *New International Version*)

Contents

1

Effective Beginnings

... getting acquainted

When your class walks in the door for the first time, you will quickly notice differences. Some come bounding in, full of enthusiasm and noise. Others are quiet and sit down quickly, waiting for you to make the first move. You will notice other differences as well—hair colors, heights, and body features. They are not the same, even though your students may be about the same age.

Other differing characteristics are not so easy to identify, but are very important. As teacher-detective you will learn:

- Some class members read well; others, not at all.
- Some students have broad religious backgrounds; others, very limited.
- Some students are interested in learning; others, disinterested.

You should try to learn as much as you can about your students on the very first day. This will help you with future planning, and it shows students that you are interested in them and their needs.

If your students are old enough to read and write, you might like to ask them to complete a short personal inventory. Ask for family information, likes and dislikes, some responses to reveal attitudes, values, and learning style preferences.

Ask your students some questions about the material you will be studying in the next few weeks. Do some already know a lot about it? Do others obviously appear "lost?" Such informal questioning will give you valuable insight on the needs of your students and help you in planning specific objectives. You may discover that you will have to plan some extra activities to keep more informed students interested, and different activities to assist those who are "behind."

A simple way to get information is to ask students to tell you all they can remember about a specific Bible story. Choose one that your class should know. Observe carefully which students seem to be able to draw on a wealth of Bible background and which ones have little to contribute. True, the shy child may appear to be less informed, but this is only one of several techniques you may find helpful. If some children do not respond, you will need to use other methods to determine the reasons for their lack of response.

Another method which is often successful with younger, or shy, students is letting them use hand puppets or flannelgraph figures to tell Bible stories. This technique will also give you some idea as to which children are more familiar with religious topics.

Whatever method you use for getting to know your students, remember that the first priority of the good teacher is to get well acquainted, as quickly as possible, with his or her students.

▶ *food for thought*

There is nothing so unfair as the equal treatment of students with unequal abilities.

... what to teach

After you are acquainted with the students in your class, you are ready to ask yourself some questions about how you will proceed:

- What do I want to teach weekly? quarterly? yearly?
- What techniques will be best?
- What do the students already know?
- What past goals need to be reviewed?
- Are the goals in keeping with the abilities of my students?
- What materials do I need?

In most cases, lesson materials will be provided for your use. You will want to use them as a guide. However, it is important that you do not follow them so rigidly that you do not allow for the differences in your students. You may, at times, need to change or substitute to make a lesson more appropriate for your particular class. Make your plans carefully and thoroughly—but remain flexible! You, as teacher, are the best authority on what is right for your particular group of students, assuming you base your judgments on your knowledge of them and their needs.

... goals and objectives

Study your lesson materials for both long-range and short-term goals. It is important for every teacher, regardless of the age of the students being taught, to know exactly what it is his or her pupils should be able to do as a result of learning. To say that pupils should "understand" or "know" is vague. Such terms do not describe your goals clearly enough for your instruction to be effective.

Good teachers learn to make objectives which are descriptive of desired student performance. These are called *behavioral* objectives because they tell what the child should be able to do as the result of learning. Students are asked to demonstrate their knowledge by some specific *action.* A preschool child might be requested to describe, show, tell, or select correctly in order to demonstrate that he or she has learned. An older pupil should be able to write, match, list, order, sketch, or perform a more advanced task. Whether you are planning for individual activities, small groups, or a large group session, be sure you tell your students:

- what it is you expect them to learn
- what you will want them to do at the end of the instruction to demonstrate their learning.

You'll be amazed to find that your students will be turned on and tuned in if you let them know, *when you begin your lesson,* what they will be expected to do at the end of the instruction time. Here's a comparison for you:

OBJECTIVE 1: At the end of this lesson, you should be able to understand Paul's first missionary journey.

That's pretty indefinite, isn't it? Understand what? Where Paul went? Who went with him? His difficulties? His successes? What he taught?

The students might as well go to sleep, because the whole point of the lesson is too indefinite for them (and maybe the teacher) to know what is expected of them.

OBJECTIVE 2: At the end of this lesson, you should be able, when given an appropriate map, to draw a line showing Paul's first missionary journey and circle the places where he preached.

That clicks, doesn't it? Students will need to watch and listen in order to know what to put on that map. Their discussion will include questions pertaining to the specific objective.

While this comparison deals with a geographic skill, similar objectives might deal with additional aspects of Paul's journey:

At the end of this lesson, you should be able, when given a list of New Testament characters, to circle the names of those who traveled with Paul on his first missionary journey.

Notice that the italicized objectives tell what knowledge will be expected and what resources the student will be given in demonstrating this knowledge.

The teacher who would like to interest all of his students will try to provide ways to meet objectives. Here is one way: Try a "learning pathway" approach to help organize different learning objectives within the class.

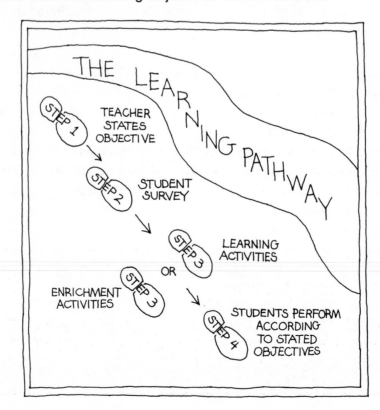

STEP 1. State the objectives in terms of student performance. New Bible-school literature is now including both long-range goals and short-term lesson performance objectives. This material makes the teacher's task easier. If your lesson does not clearly identify objectives in terms of exactly what the student is expected to do to demonstrate his knowledge, *then you must make up your own performance objectives.* Make sure the student knows exactly what he is expected to learn as the result of the class session.

STEP 2. Some advanced students may already be able to meet the objectives. A quick class survey in the form of a game-like quiz or class discussion will show you which students need enrichment activities. Be careful if a discussion is used, that you don't make the mistake of assuming that shy students who do not respond are less advanced. If you have difficulty drawing out students like this, include some written responses. *This is an important step.* It is vital to your planning for individual and group activities.

STEP 3. This step provides learning activities to help students perform the stated objectives. It provides alternate enrichment activities for those students who have already mastered the objectives. This is an excellent time to plan which learning center activities may suit the needs of your class. Some teachers may wish to plan for three groups at this point—one for enrichment activities, one for the regular lesson, and another for easier activities to suit those who may have a great deal of difficulty meeting the lesson objectives. While much of the Bible-school literature includes ideas for enrichment activities, you may have to do your own "simplifying" for less advanced students.

STEP 4. Students are asked to perform according to the stated objectives. Groups will often like to report to one another on their activities. This may be a part of the performance evaluation.

The "learning pathway" approach will help you plan more effectively. Keep these two purposes in mind:

1. Provide effective learning activities for those who do not have prior knowledge so that they may gain new skills and understandings.
2. Provide enrichment activities for those who already have such skills and understandings.

▶ *food for thought*

Several different learning activities for teaching the same objective will increase the possibility of learning . . . one approach might not "take," but the next one may.

ADULT APPLICATION. The idea of the "learning pathway" has been used successfully with adult classes. Teachers of adult classes are often amazed to discover the extent of prior knowledge possessed by their students. This is discovered when the pretest is given. Results of the pretest may lead the adult teacher to:

- Include more background material if class members are weak in needed prerequisite knowledge.
- Omit some material, if the adult students already have mastered the content.
- Provide class members with suggested home study ideas for the purpose of enrichment, or providing needed background information.

Adult students respond very well when they observe a teacher making a systematic and concerned effort to meet their learning needs. Remember, adults also differ in their abilities, backgrounds, and learning styles!

Having studied the "learning pathway" we may now put together these two questions:

1. What do the students already know?
2. What past goals need to be reviewed?

Carefully following such a technique as Step 2 (the student survey) will help you with both of these problems. *It cannot be overemphasized how important it is for the teacher to determine the answers to these questions.* This step is vital for the teacher who wishes to meet individual needs.

We are not *teaching* students who have already met our objectives! We must plan and use enrichment lessons to help them expand their knowledge.

We are not *teaching* students for whom the goals are too advanced to be mastered! For them, we must plan review lessons or simpler applications for our present objectives.

Hurrah for the average student! He or she is right where we expect him or her to be and for this student our objectives and activities are perfect. Watch out, however, for the same students are not "average" on every lesson. It is important that you survey for each new set of goals. The experience and background of your students will vary according to the topic you are studying.

It is equally important that you remain flexible as your students begin to work. Observe them carefully. If they are not working or listening, the task may be too difficult or too simple. If they can do the lesson easily with a little "pushing," the task may be too simple to challenge them. If they can't do it no matter how much you assist, it's too hard. Adapt your techniques! Try something else!

▶ *food for thought*

If you want to find out what "turns on" your pupils, watch what they do when you don't tell them what to do.

... help for first-day jitters

Getting started with a class is often the most difficult part of teaching. The first few minutes are not only the hardest, but may be the most crucial of the year with your class.

Here are a few simple tips to help you feel more confident on the first day you meet your class.

things to do before the first day:

1. Decorate your classroom. If you have only an area within a larger room, make an interesting display for your bulletin board. If you do not have a bulletin board, make your display on poster board and tack it onto a stand-up cardboard frame (you can make this from a box) or easel.

Also consider, depending on the space available:

Pictures	Flowers or plants
Books on a table	Maps
An interest center	A seasonal display

2. Plan your classroom arrangement carefully. Have the table and chairs all ready. Put students' names on stand-up cards on the tables, or attach them to the chairs. Remember to print names if your students are under eight years old. This preparation will avoid the confusion of arranging chairs and tables on the first day.

3. Even if you do not regularly have an assistant, *enlist a helper for the first day.* A good friend, your mother or grandmother, your husband, teenage son or daughter, the butcher, the baker, or the candlestick maker may be prospects! Approach this as a *very important* part of your first day. This assistant will have two very important tasks on the first day, which will be described later.

If you exhaust all possibilities, and are unable to secure a first-day assistant, plan to have something very simple to do at the table. The activity must be so easy that your students can get busy on it while you are occupied at the door greeting students and parents as they arrive. What you plan will, of course, depend on the age of your students. It might be:

An easy puzzle	A name tag to make
Crayons and something to color	A personal survey to complete
Books to look at	The information card to complete

Whatever you plan, *keep it simple.* Do not end up with a lot of toys or art materials to put away before you can begin your class session. It is important, especially on the first day, to get the students to their seats and quickly involved in a simple, quiet activity. This makes them more comfortable and will avoid problems for you.

4. Plan every detail of your first class session. Make sure you have all needed materials.

• Several days ahead, read your printed lesson material if it is provided for you. If it is not provided, decide on a theme or story for your first day. (This is a good point at which to request printed lesson material if it is not provided. It will help you do a better job for your students.)

• Plan your get-acquainted activity and make all needed visual aids.

• Be sure you have needed supplies for your students—crayons, pencils, paper, glue, etc. Think through each step of your session and list what will be needed. Don't count on anyone else providing what you need. Get it yourself—ahead of time!

5. Prepare an information card for parents or relatives of younger children to complete on the first day. Search out a small table, desk, or stand to put in the hall, slightly away from your door to avoid congestion. Plan to put your cards and a supply of pencils (in an attractive little jar or decorated can, please!) there for parents' use. Your information card may look like this:

```
┌─────────────────────────────────────────────────────┐
│ Child's name _____ │
│ Parent's name _____ │
│ Address _____ │
│ Phone number _____ │
│ Brought by: (if not parent) _____ │
│ Emergency contact during school time: _____ │
│   Name_____Location _____ │
└─────────────────────────────────────────────────────┘
```

This example shows how a card might be completed on a Sunday morning. If you have a weekday school, your information may be more detailed. The emergency contact might be an older relative, a friend, or the driver of a church bus, but *be sure you get this information.* If a child becomes ill or injured, it is invaluable to you. Be aware that some younger children become ill on the *first* day due to excitement or fear, so this is an especially important part of your first-day's preparation. *Insist* that the card be completed by the person bringing a younger child to your class. It is best not to let the relative take it home and send it back the following week. This will not help you if you have a problem on the first day and it also prevents any follow-up contacts on first-time visitors the first week. Children over age seven can usually give you this information, or complete the card themselves, as a part of your initial class session.

6. Be sure you have a clock in your room, or plan to wear a watch.
7. Try to have a United States flag and a Christian flag in your classroom.

things to do on the first day:

1. Arrive at your classroom at least thirty minutes early. Check to be sure that your arrangements, made the previous day (or several days ago), are still in good order. Put out your name tags on tables, or attach to chairs.

2. Stand at the door of your room and look *at your room.* Does it look attractive and inviting? Does it look neat and well organized? Try to see your room as it will look to the students and parents who will look at it for the first time in a few minutes. Are you satisfied?

3. Be at your door to greet each child (and parent) as they arrive. Be friendly with parents, but center your attention on the child and avoid a lengthy conversation with the relative who accompanies him or her. Know exactly what you want your new students to do, and tell them clearly after you greet them. You might say, "After you hang up your coat, John (or Susan), you may find your place at the table and sit down. You'll find something interesting there to do until I can join you."

Hopefully, you will have enlisted an aide to assist you on this special, first day. The aide should be well instructed and able to help children carry out this preliminary project.

If parents are anxious to talk to you, assure them that you will call them. Ask, "When is the best time for me to call you? I'd like to discuss this when we have more time."

Direct the parent or relative of younger children (under age seven) to the table you have prepared and ask that the information card be completed.

4. When it is time to start class, trade places with your aide. You should go to the table with your students, while the aide goes *outside* the classroom door to greet latecomers. This will accomplish three important things:

a. Your students will know that you are well prepared and that you start on time.

b. Parents or relatives who bring children will learn that you start on time.

c. It will avoid confusion and interruptions as you start your class. If you do not have an aide, make a small sign to put on the outside of your door as your "substitute:"

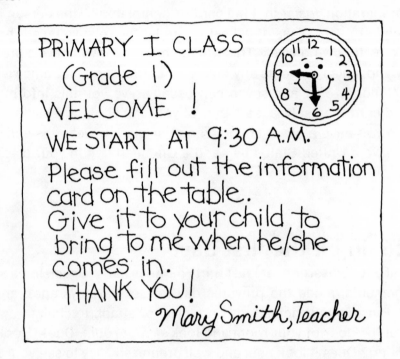

5. Your first comments to your class, of course, will depend on their age. Regardless of age, however, in an appropriate way, you will want to get across these things:

a. You are enthusiastic and happy to be with them as their teacher.

b. You want to get to know them well so you can help them learn.

c. You want them to know you as a friend and helper, and as someone who likes them.

d. You have definite standards of behavior based on courtesy and consideration for others.

e. *You* have planned many special and interesting activities to help them learn. It will be their responsibility to enter into these activities and help *themselves* to learn.

It is sometimes fun to use a simple chalk talk (or large paper with a black marker) to introduce yourself. Draw some blank circles on your blackboard:

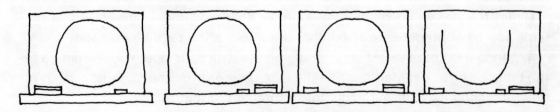

"I'm a blank to you now, like these circles. I have already told you my name, and you can see my name tag *(be sure to wear one!),* but you may wonder what I am really like. Maybe you think I will be mean or cross, . . . (Complete first circle.)

"Or, perhaps, you think I will talk all the time . . . (Complete second circle.)

"Or, will I be fun to be with, and happy all the time? . . ." (Complete third circle.)

"I will plan lots of interesting things and do my best to have good lessons for you. You will have to do your best to try to learn and help me to do a good job. If you do this, I will be like the last face . . . so, you see, it is really up to . . ." (Enlarge and shade in the mouth on last figure.)

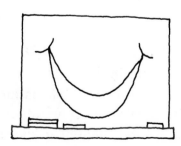

6. You have told your students what they can expect you to do. Put these on the board, or a chart, as you repeat them:

Next, ask students to tell you what they think their job will be. Below is a sample of suggestions from boys and girls. Try to get agreement from your students on three or four items after you have listed all of their suggestions. Make a final chart, using their ideas:

Let parents know that both you and the students have agreed upon your individual responsibilities. Give them copies of your charts, and ask them to suggest a few responsibilities for parents. Compile these and complete a parent's responsibilities chart. Make all three charts as neat and attractive as you can and display them near your room door. They will serve as a reminder for parents and students that you take your teaching seriously, and expect them to do so, too. Review these often with your students the first few weeks. Getting started well means letting students (and parents) know what is expected. Try this—it works!

7. After your instructions are completed, it is important to have some actual work ready for the students to complete and carry home on the first day! For the "body" of your first lesson, distribute and examine together the materials the students will be using. Give them an idea of what their future activities and lessons will be. Be sure you explain the schedule you will follow each time your class meets. Tell them about learning centers or other areas of the room.

If it was not completed earlier, be sure to have students complete the information card and the personal survey (see preceding samples).

8. Check your list to be sure you are ready. If you have made good preparations, your first day will be over quickly and you will have:

- arrived early to check your room
- greeted students and parents
- established your starting time with students and parents
- received information cards for emergency use and future contacts of pupils
- introduced yourself
- established behavior and learning expectations
- introduced your daily schedule and classroom areas
- had students complete the personal inventory
- sent students home with some work or paper completed

If you did not manage to complete the entire list, don't be discouraged. It is always better to plan more than can be done than to underplan! Any of these activities can be continued into the second or third lesson. The important thing is for you to know what you wish to accomplish and continue to move in that direction.

▶ *food for thought*

A teacher's classroom is a reflection of his/her own personality. Look at your classroom. What do you think of yourself?

2

Effective Planning

. . . know where you're going

After you have established your objectives and made them known to your students, you face the problem of determining how to meet them. It is one thing to say, "At the end of this year you will be able to recite the names of the books of the Bible," and another matter to plan activities that will help students meet this goal! Even assuming that now you know your students well enough to establish *realistic* objectives, planning activities can be a challenge.

Extensive research has been done in order to determine what type of environment, what teaching techniques, and what kinds of activities are most effective in helping students to learn. We will keep this in mind as we discuss again individualizing as a basic consideration in good planning. Remember, individualization, meeting individual needs, may include the physical surroundings—the classroom itself: light, heat, color, furniture arrangement—and a wide range of teacher and pupil activities. Some of these are:

1. *Know your students.* It is vital to know your pupils well. Visit in their homes. Learn their hobbies, habits, and family relationships. Know about their religious backgrounds and their attitudes toward God and the church. Never fall into the misconception that you, a mature, ethical, loving teacher, will be "prejudiced" by learning all you can about your students. The good teacher will never misuse this information. It is a basic necessity for teaching each student as an *individual!*

2. *Use a variety of activities.* Research tells us that some students learn best alone or on independent projects. Others are adult oriented or teacher centered

and need the motivation of these to learn well. Still others learn best from peers or friends. Keeping this in mind, it is best to plan activities in which students can be allowed to work alone, with others, or with close supervision.

3. *Provide a variety of learning resources.* The majority of your students will be visual learners. This means they will learn best through looking at something to reinforce instruction. Pictures, filmstrips, graphs, blackboard illustrations, books, flannelgraph, and puppets all meet this need. A smaller percentage of your students will learn best through auditory (listening) activities. For them, you should plan activities that include tapes, records, simple stories, or lectures without visuals. It is also important to remember that the majority of your students who appear to have difficulties with learning are those who will need tactile (touchable) learning aids. For them, manipulative materials such as puzzles, flannelgraph figures, hand puppets, or models will be invaluable.

4. *Teach as a resource person and helper.* Adopt the role of a guide in learning, providing materials and the amount of direction needed for your students. State goals and objectives clearly, explain assignments and activities, and then give your students some options in how to carry out your instructions. Don't smother your students with teacher talk when they are ready to get on with a task. Keep those who seem to need more direction close to you and give them the added supervision they need, but remember that some students will prefer working alone or with peers, and are self-directed.

5. *Communicate with individuals.* The good teacher knows that broad, general messages often go unheard. Talk as much as you can with individuals or small groups.

6. *Vary your questioning techniques.* Endeavor to phrase your questions so they are varied in type and difficulty. Some students will respond best to simple, cognitive, or recall questions. These will begin with:

> Who?
> What?
> Where?
> When?

Usually these questions can be answered with one or two words and involve only simple thought processes. More capable students will respond to questions of a higher (divergent) level. These may start with:

> What?
> Why?
> How?

Leading students to compare, explain, or evaluate should be the ultimate goal of every good teacher.

7. *Evaluate frequently and individually.* Finding out what your students know is essential to determining if learning is taking place. Are they meeting the objectives? If the answer is yes, you must move on to the next set of objectives to avoid boredom. If the answer is no, you should determine why and plan different types of activities, or revise your objectives. Only through continual

evaluation can you be certain your students are learning and will continue to learn!

8. *Have a lesson plan, but be flexible.* Plans are vital, but they must at times be changed. You may find, as mentioned above, that your objectives are not appropriate. Perhaps it develops that they are too easy or too difficult for your pupils. Back up, and make some new, realistic objectives. Perhaps you need more time than you had planned. If the objectives are good and pupils are learning, take more time. Pupils may vary greatly in the amount of time needed to complete tasks. Allow for this in your planning. Individualizing, remember, will provide for both extra time and extra help for students.

Are you beginning to realize that individualization in learning does not mean one child working all by himself? Most children learn best when working with someone else or in a small group. It is the important task of the teacher to carefully plan the total learning "package." This includes environment, goals, objectives, the combination of pupils working on a task, and the instructional activity assigned.

Many excellent teachers use "job cards" or "activity cards" as a method for planning learning experiences. Each card carries a symbol for quick identification:

$\perp$ individual activity

$\triangle$ small group, 2-5 students

$\bigcirc$ large group, entire class

Example cards:

Activity: Listen to cassette story #4.　　　　$\perp$ $\triangle$

Goal: To give examples of everyday applications of the Golden Rule.

Performance Objective: After hearing the tape you should be able to identify correctly four sentences from the tape which describe everyday applications of the Golden Rule.

Suggestion: Discuss the examples on the tape in your small group before asking the teacher for your quiz.

Activity: Use your Bible to look up references.

Goal: To identify materials used in Solomon's temple.

Performance Objective: List the materials given in each of these Scriptures, used in Solomon's temple: 1 Kings 6:30; 1 Kings 6:36; 1 Kings 7:9; 1 Kings 7:15.

Suggestion: Work alone, or with a partner, to look up the Scriptures and list the materials. Tell the teacher when you think you have them all.

Activity cards should tell what resources or materials the student will need, as well as what he will be expected to do when he has completed the activity.

Additional ideas for activities will be found in following chapters. You will not always be able to select the perfect goals or activities, or have the ideal classroom environment for each individual. Such a level of perfection is not achieved by even the most experienced teachers. But the fact that you cannot achieve perfection should never keep you from striving to improve!

▶ *food for thought*

Our purpose should be to equip students with the skills, tools, and motivation to become lifelong Christians with a lifelong commitment.

... teach essential skills

The essential skills for your students are whatever skills they need to understand and learn what you are teaching. You, as teacher, have important and often very broad responsibilities. The first step in carrying out these responsibilities is to be sure that the student has the skills and understands what is expected of him or her. The teacher who gives a student written activities containing directions that he cannot read, and then complains because the student does not complete the task, is not worthy of the name "teacher." Regardless of whether you are teaching public school social studies, Christian doctrine, or Bible history, it is your responsibility to provide your students with the "tools" necessary for them to learn. These include:

teach the needed vocabulary

Students who do poor work almost always have very limited vocabularies. Select the important words from your lessons and introduce them to your students:

- put the new words on the board or a chart
- define the word or tell about the person
- use the word in a sentence
- ask students to use the word
- use pictures to create visual images of the new words
- have students make dictionaries of new words
- make up games to use including the new words

teach students how to listen

Almost every aspect of the teaching program calls for good listening habits. Stories, dramas, recordings, music, films, announcements, and discussion groups all necessitate listening skills. The good teacher remembers that the vast majority of her pupils learn best through *looking* rather than listening and provides help with listening skills.

Listening is, in some respects, a more difficult process to master than reading. The listener has no control over the rate at which he must listen; nor does he have a page before him so he can go back and reexamine ideas. Further, the language to which he listens is not always as well organized, or as suitable to his level of understanding, as that which he reads.

When a child enters school he has already had a considerable amount of experience in listening. However, he must be taught to listen accurately, purposefully, and responsively. Situations in which the child needs to listen effectively begin in the preschool departments and increase in number and intensity as the student proceeds through the elementary years. Even adult students often benefit from instruction in listening techniques. The teacher must first consider:

The physical factors in the classroom: distractions in the room, people moving about, noises from the street, all may hinder good listening. Make every effort to provide a classroom that is conducive to effective listening.

Possible hearing defects of students: any student with a hearing problem should be seated in the best position for hearing. As often as possible be certain the hearing impaired student can see the teacher's face.

teaching techniques to foster good listening

1. Develop listening readiness by relating the material to previous experiences of pupils, teaching the meaning of new words, and asking stimulating

questions. Creating an interest in the topic to be studied will greatly raise the listening level of your students.

2. Help students develop a purpose for listening. This may be to find answers to questions, reasons for the occurrence of events, or to find flaws in an argument. Making sure that students know what they are expected to learn will provide a focus for their listening.

3. Be sure that the spoken material suits the maturity level, the attention span, and the previous experiences of your students.

4. Help students to verbally summarize at the end of a lesson.

5. Give students assistance in evaluating what they have heard. They need to learn to differentiate fact and opinion, half-truths and false claims. Are stories you tell true or fictitious? When using "make believe" characters with young children, be sure they understand when you "shift gears" to a Bible story describing real people and events.

6. Teach pupils of all ages the importance of courteous listening. This is a practical application of the Golden Rule. It is often best taught by your example. Do not talk when others are talking. If students are conversing, wait quietly until they are attentive. Be sure that if a student is talking to you personally or to the class as a whole that you, the teacher, are an attentive listener. Courteous listening is essential for effective group relationships.

teach about numbers

Numbering the people was common in Old Testament times. In the New Testament we study about the famous census taking that led Mary and Joseph to Bethlehem. Jesus used many illustrations referring to numbers. How much do your students understand about counting and numbers? You cannot become involved in teaching detailed mathematics skills to your students, but it is your responsibility to teach them the needed vocabulary to understand your subject area. The language of mathematics is a part of Biblical teaching. Be sure you remember to:

1. Become acquainted with the mathematical concepts appropriate for your students. Simple concepts such as before, after, under, above, first, and last may be new to some kindergarten children. Explain and illustrate new concepts.

2. Use concrete or visual examples as often as possible. Mathematical concepts are more readily grasped when students can handle an object or see an illustration.

3. Explain unfamiliar measurement and monetary terminology, such as:

span (the width from the end of the thumb to that of the little finger, when these were extended—about 9 inches; 23 centimeters)

cubit (the length of the arm from the point of the elbow to the end of the middle finger—about 18 inches; 46 centimeters)

Sabbath Day's journey (two thousand cubits—about 3/5 of a mile or 1 kilometer)

omer (5.1 pints; 1/10 ephah; 4 liters)

ephah (10 omers; 1.1 bushel; 40 liters)

denarius (about 44 cents today)

shekel (.134 ounces; 3.8 grams)

mite (small coin of little value)

talent (3000 shekels; 75 pounds; 34.02 kilograms)

teach geographical concepts

As we keep in mind that every teacher teaches basic skills, we must realize the importance of the study of geography as we teach about the Bible. Our Biblical literature is filled with names of locations. One of the most exciting realizations for your students will be finding out that these are *real places* that can be located on a map, photographed, painted by artists, and even visited. Every classroom for school-age children or adults should have appropriate maps. It is not difficult to realize the need for maps when reading about the journeys of the apostle Paul. This same need should be felt when reading about Moses, Jesus, and other Biblical characters. Whenever possible, show photographs or slides of locations mentioned. Older students will appreciate artists' renditions of Biblical scenes. The old adage, "a picture is worth a thousand words," is as appropriate in the geographical area as it is in learning about people. A mental picture of an area also helps students better understand the factors affecting the everyday life of people. Verbal descriptions such as "rocky hillside," "hot, dry land," or "beautiful Sea of Galilee" become much more meaningful if accompanied by pictures and maps.

It is important to remember that the good teacher teaches every skill that is needed to help students learn the lesson being taught. The good teacher continually teaches the basics!

... share your good work

In schools and churches we may call it communication. In the business world it is called public relations. Whatever name we give it, it is important to make known our good work to those outside our class. It motivates the students by creating interest from others in what they are doing, as well as providing parents with a means of sharing in the learning process at home. Here are ten ideas for communicating that have proven successful:

1. Develop a month by month planned program of varied communication ideas. Plan to use at least one idea each month.

2. Have a monthly or quarterly newsletter to send home with students. Give

the teacher's name, introduce new members, recognize the achievements of students and teachers, give an outline of what you will be studying, and publicize your coming projects and activities.

3. Appoint or enlist some class "room mothers" to assist with preparing communications, telephoning, or greeting at the door. (This can be an excellent way to spot potential teachers.)

4. Invite parents to visit your class. Ideas used have been "Grandparent's Day," "Mom's Day," "Dad's Day," etc.

5. Have a planned program to meet visitors. Decide in advance who will be the door greeter, who gets the next new student, who makes the home visit or "welcome" follow-up phone call, who will send a special "welcome" letter.

6. Develop a special packet of material to send home with first time visitors. Possibilities for this include sample lesson papers, department goals, monthly lesson objectives, welcome greeting signed by the teacher, etc.

7. Use an attractive, well-made message poster outside your class door. This can be a door bulletin board or stand on an easel. Take instant pictures of your class and put them on the bulletin board as visual messages of your activities for parents and others to see.

8. Have a family picnic for your class. While children play games (planned by teachers or aides) have a short session with parents and explain your teaching goals.

9. Have an "Alumni Day" for former students. Invite them to visit your room. Students may like to present a short skit and serve refreshments.

10. Schedule regular planning time to communicate with other teachers and plan your class sessions. On Sunday mornings, or during weekday classes, use your time to communicate with students.

▶ *food for thought*

Most things done in Bible schools after age five have a relationship to reading. Time spent helping children or older students learn to read Bible words is not time wasted.

3

Effective Techniques

Effective teaching is not complicated. It is straightforward and always well planned. It takes understanding, gained either through teacher training, experience, or intuition about human nature, of the developmental characteristics of children and how they learn. Every good teacher follows some procedures common to all other good teachers. These procedures or techniques have been identified in many and varied research projects and extensively studied. The important thing to remember is that they are not complicated and can be learned. *If you follow the procedures of good teachers, you can become a good teacher.* Keep in mind that it takes advance planning, hard work, and practice, as is true of quality performance in any field of endeavor.

. . . if you must lecture

Lecturing is the most common method of teaching. A lecture can be a highly effective technique or extremely poor, depending on the way it is delivered. We recognize that teachers must talk to students. However, the effective teacher realizes that it takes much more than talking to bring about meaningful thinking on the part of students. To become a learning experience thought must be transferred into some type of action. Oscar Hammerstein wrote:

"A song is not a song
until you sing it."

This could be paraphrased in regard to the thinking process:

"A thought is not a thought
until you write or speak it."

Thoughts or ideas do not become truly firm for the learner until they are used in some physical way. Albert Einstein, one of the 20th century's greatest intellects, recognized this when he wrote:

"The psychical entities which seem to serve as *elements of thought* are of a visual and muscular nature."

The wise teacher learns to tap student energy as a part of every lecture. He helps students to put their thoughts into some physical form. The teacher does not wear himself out doing all the work while students sit idly, bored, or active doing all the wrong things. Chart A illustrates how student energy can be diverted away from the teacher's lesson, if the need for physical involvement is not met:

CHART A

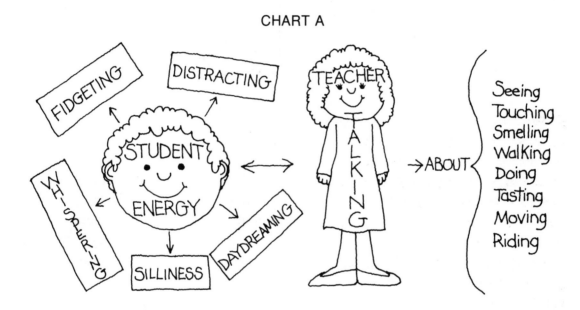

When students are asked to sit and listen with no activity involved, their excess energy, as illustrated, is shifted into many nonlearning activities. These activities can develop into discipline problems (see Chapter 5) depending on the nature and age of the students. The good teacher learns, however, through teacher-education classes, experience, or intuition that the first principle for both effective learning and good discipline is to keep the students busy. This principle applies even in the lecture situation. Students must be provided with ample ways to use their energy (Chart B).

When effective teachers lecture, they continually involve their students as active participants by providing them with guided activities to reinforce their words and the students' thoughts. Good teachers frequently use verbs that require student responses. Following are several lists of various types of verbs, many of which should become a part of your vocabulary as you speak to students. These words will suggest to you the many types of activities in which you can involve your students.

Teacher Guided
Seeing
Touching
Smelling
Hearing
Moving
Tasting
Doing
Writing
Speaking

general study-skill verbs

chart	follow	map	place
choose	identify	mark	quote
circle	indicate	match	record
cite	itemize	name	select
copy	label	omit	separate
define	list	order	sort
describe	locate	organize	underline
find	look	pick	

creative activity verbs

alter	paraphrase	restate
ask	predict	retell
change	rearrange	revise
design	rename	rewrite
generalize	regroup	synthesize
modify	reorder	systematize

complex-higher level thinking activity verbs

analyze	contrast	evaluate	plan
appraise	criticize	explain	structure
combine	decide	formulate	substitute
compare	deduce	induce	
conclude	defend	infer	

social behavior activity verbs

accept	communicate	excuse	join
agree	compliment	forgive	laugh
aid	contribute	greet	meet
allow	cooperate	help	praise
answer	disagree	interest	talk
argue	discuss	invite	thank

language activity verbs

alphabetize	punctuate	summarize
call	read	tell
capitalize	recite	translate
outline	speak	verbalize
print	spell	whisper
pronounce	state	write

The teacher who wishes to involve students as active participants in the learning process, helping them to put their thoughts into action, uses many of these words during a lecture. Keeping these words in mind will help you call for active participation on the part of your students.

. . . vary your stimulus

Have you ever tried to identify the differences between a teacher who keeps students interested every minute and the one who puts pupils to sleep? If you have you most likely noticed that the stimulating teacher uses many of the following techniques:

1. *Movement.* This teacher keeps student attention by moving about the room. He walks from the front to the back of the room, sits down, or walks down the middle. He does not remain in one location behind a desk, podium, or table for very long, but takes advantage of movement as a simple way to increase student attention.

2. *Focusing and gestures.* This teacher makes an effort to gain student attention through meaningful gestures or pointing. She points to locations on a map, underlines, circles, or checks statements on the board or a chart to guide pupils' eyes and focus their attention on important points. She may use hand movements or "acting out" gestures as effective attention-getters. These are subtle but notable characteristics of many good teachers.

3. *Change of interaction styles.* This teacher uses communication within the class in various ways. The most commonly used interaction style in adult

classes is *teacher-group interaction.* In this, the teacher lectures to the entire group, asking questions or giving directions to the group at large. The questions will commonly be answered by the teacher or by a show of hands. The next most frequently used presentation method is *teacher-student interaction.* This teacher lectures the group but directs questions to specific students, sometimes discussing a point in detail with one student. Problems can arise in this type of presentation if there is a student who is inclined to dominate the class. This is avoided if the teacher changes the interaction style. An effective but less often used interaction style is the *student-student technique.* In this class the teacher may take one student's response and direct it to another student for comment or clarification. Another variation is for one student to explain something to another student. In this setting the teacher takes the "back seat" temporarily allowing student interactions to occur. The good teacher knows the value of changing from one interaction style to another as a method of keeping student interest.

4. *Pausing.* This teacher has learned the value of a pause in effective teaching. It is difficult to overestimate the importance of this technique. Pauses are of extreme value after key teacher statements or questions. Time is needed for students to absorb information and for them to consider responses to questions.

Studies have indicated that both the number of responses and the quality of responses increase when teachers wait longer for students to reply. How long are your pauses? Few teachers allow more than one or two seconds for students to respond to questions before either answering them themselves or rephrasing the question. Force yourself to become a "three-second pause" teacher! Avoid rushing in to fill silent spaces with talk or activity. Effective teachers have learned to wait five or even ten seconds for student responses. They have learned the value of waiting!

5. *Shift sensory channels.* This teacher knows that he cannot talk, talk, talk, and expect students to do little but listen, listen, listen. The sense of hearing is the one we expect our students to use constantly. Hearing is important, but whenever possible we will increase our teaching effectiveness when we add another "sense." Visual messages can be sent by using the chalkboard, pictures, maps, overhead projectors, slides, or charts. When it is appropriate, try to include a tactile message by passing around an object to handle or allow students to manipulate some apparatus.

The effective teacher has learned to frequently shift from one sensory channel to another within every lesson. He varies the listening mode by using recorded messages or having someone else speak or read at times. He will add a visual image via the chalkboard, a simple sheet of paper on which he has written a few words or drawn a diagram, a filmstrip, or an overhead projector. He sometimes forces the student to use the visual, sensory channel without using spoken words. Written words, charts, and pictures may be used without spoken comments by the teacher, forcing the student to shift to the visual, sensory channel and increasing the effectiveness of the visual aid being used.

6. *Reinforcement.* Simply stated, this teacher has learned the effectiveness of letting students know when they do or say the right thing. This is a valuable teaching technique! This teacher, through verbal or nonverbal acceptance of students, establishes a comfortable classroom atmosphere. This teacher makes students feel at ease and gives them the impression that he or she is continually "on their side." He may smile, nod, pat a student on the back, or comment such as, "That's a very good thought," or "I like the way you stated that." Even the incorrect response does not bring about a "put-down" but may receive a comment such as, "You have a thought there, John. Would anyone like to add to this idea?" It is never necessary to praise errors, but the student who willingly endeavors to participate can be praised and encouraged for his or her efforts. The good teacher develops a wide vocabulary of words and phrases of praise and encouragement.

. . . beginnings and endings

These are such important techniques, they deserve special attention. While a good beginning and ending will not make a *complete* lesson, they are essential to the *effective* lesson.

the beginning

A good introduction, or beginning, is a well planned part of your lesson. You should allow up to one-fourth of your time for it. Introductory remarks, to be meaningful, must be more extensive than: "Today we will learn about the good Samaritan." or "Open your Bible to the first chapter in the book of John."

The purpose of the introduction is to set the mood, motivate interest, arouse curiosity, or state objectives for the listening that is to follow. The teacher may wish to ask some questions to be answered throughout the lesson to follow. She may tell an unusual story related to the lesson or display an interest-creating object or picture. The following characteristics of a good beginning may be helpful as you plan this vital part of your lesson:

1. *Refer to past or future lessons.* Make an effort to tie the current lesson with what was taught last week, yesterday, or at some other time in the past. Relate the lesson to what will be learned in the future. Tell how the knowledge may be helpful to the student. Use such statements as, "You may remember that last week we learned about . . ." "Today we will carry this idea one step further as we study . . ." "When we begin to study . . . in next week's lesson it will be helpful if you have learned . . . (what we will study today) . . ."

Relate what is being learned to the general knowledge of students by the use of such statements as, "You will remember that at the time of Jesus Christ,

Jerusalem was under Roman rule. In today's lesson you will see why (what, how, when). . . ."

2. *Tell students what you expect them to learn in this lesson.* Be specific. Be sure they know exactly what knowledge you want them to gain. Many research studies have shown that students who are told learning objectives in advance of the lesson *learn more* than those who are not informed. It cannot be emphasized enough that this should be a part of every lesson. Students will take a greater interest in learning and learn more if they know what they are expected to learn. At the beginning of each lesson write on the chalkboard or a large sheet of paper what it is that the student will learn that day. State it simply, using some of the active verbs given previously (on page 32). Your statement might use these words:

"At the end of this lesson you should be able to

IDENTIFY . . . .

TELL . . . .

LIST . . . .

DESCRIBE . . . ."

It is also helpful to tell students what the activities will be. Will they need Bibles? notebooks? paper and pencil? Will they be looking at a filmstrip, chart, map, or poster? Knowing these things in advance makes students more interested and attentive. You will also avoid interruptions from younger children who see various articles in the room and are curious about them. Knowing what to expect has a calming effect on students and will help put the excitable or timid ones at ease.

3. *Refer to the introduction as you move through the lesson.* While this technique is not a part of the introduction, it has an important relationship to it. Once having stated objectives, it is important to ask simple questions related to them as you continue your lesson. Asking simple recall questions will help keep all students interested, while leading more advanced students to be ready to respond to higher level questions as you conclude your lesson. Encourage students to raise their hands, or otherwise signal, when they are aware of a learning objective having been met. This may then be marked on the board, chart, or student outlines.

the ending

While it may be an exaggeration, it has been said that a meal with a tasty, delicious dessert will seem to be perfect. This is somewhat true of an effective lesson. If you have a good beginning (introduction) and a meaningful ending (conclusion), your lesson has a better chance of being remembered. The skill of concluding involves drawing the lesson to an effective end. Too often, a teacher's conclusion is simply, "Next week we will study the book of Acts," or "That's all for today." A meaningful conclusion should be planned as carefully as the beginning and body of the lesson. It may include:

- Relating the lesson back to the original objectives.
- Reviewing major points covered by the class during the lesson.
- Reviewing the sequence that was followed in moving from known to new material.
- Applying the Bible teachings learned to everyday examples or illustrations.
- Allowing pupils to summarize what has been learned, giving their examples.
- Reviewing the activities and relating them to the lesson objectives.
- Helping students to see what has been presented as the basis for future studies.
- Telling students what will be included in the next lesson.

. . . gifted and handicapped

What special techniques will you need for "exceptional" children—the extremes of the intellectual and ability range? After a number of years of efforts to remove the learning disabled (slow learner, retarded, or emotionally disturbed), handicapped (crippled, hearing or visually impaired), or gifted (intellectually or creatively superior) child from the classroom into segregated classes designed to meet their special needs, the trend today is to "mainstream." Mainstreaming is an effort to keep the student with his or her age group as much of the time as possible, removing him or her from the group only to meet the most severe needs. Such students are sometimes tutored on a one-to-one basis, or placed in small interest or ability groups with teachers trained to meet their special needs. Few Christian schools have had special classes, so mainstreaming will be viewed as "what has been done all along." Efforts have been made, and should continue to be made, for these children within the regular classroom framework.

Some special considerations should be made, however, for each of these students as you prepare to meet their individual needs. If you have such students, you will wish to look for additional resources, such as *77 Dynamic Ideas for the Christian Education of the Handicapped* by James Pierson. (Available from Standard, #7970.)

Much has been written about the identification, characteristics, and needs of exceptional children. It is not our purpose to go into great detail regarding them in this book, but as we consider effective teaching some basic considerations should be made. As for every student in your class, provision must be made to meet the individual needs of the one who is not "typical" or "average."

gifted students

The gifted student is one who is usually identified as gifted because of superior intellectual ability. However, the U.S. Department of Education has identified four areas of "giftedness." These are:

- Intellectual superiority
- Superior creative ability
- Outstanding social skills (i.e., leadership)
- Physically superior (outstanding skill in one or many physical activities)

The teacher may not have tests to confirm giftedness, but here are some guidelines that have been used:

. . . The gifted student grasps ideas more quickly than other students.

. . . The gifted student understands subtle humor that other students miss.

. . . The gifted student moves to higher level thinking quickly, often skipping more routine facts. He or she may ask probing questions or respond easily to questions necessitating comparisons, concluding, summarizing, or imagination.

. . . The gifted student may come up with unusual or unexpected responses. When analyzed, these responses show creative thinking or depth of thought.

. . . The gifted student often performs skills well above the usual accomplishments for his or her age group. He or she may read much better than others, or grasp number concepts beyond the normal for their age group. While handwriting or spelling may be careless, the gifted child will think through tasks, understand them, and finish quickly.

. . . The gifted student may excel in some particular area—outstanding achievement in music, writing, or a physical skill.

. . . The gifted student *may* be advanced in social skills and more mature. However, this does not mean that he or she will relate well to his or her own age group. He may have trouble understanding why others do not see things as he does. She may become impatient and a discipline problem if her needs are not understood and met. This student can also become introverted and nonparticipating if unusual or advanced responses are resented. Usually the bright child will learn to compensate for differences and try hard to be socially acceptable, but often will relate best to older students or adults.

It is important for the teacher to plan some activities to challenge and interest the gifted child. We must be careful not to let the gifted child become the class janitor by giving him or her too many "housekeeping" tasks because assigned work is finished quickly and easily. The gifted child may help others from time to time, but it is also important to have extra games, books, and learning centers which will be a challenge when assignments are completed. Even though the gifted child may know how to do many things above the level of other students, he or she still needs and deserves to learn as a result of our teaching.

The gifted student may enjoy taking notes or researching special topics to report to the class. Surveying other students or adults about interests or attitudes is often challenging to the bright student. The possibility of moving the gifted student to an advanced class may be considered, but this should be done with much thought and caution if the student is happy in his or her present setting. Temporary advancement for a special lesson or series of lessons may provide an alternative to permanent advancement. The use of resource persons or a mentor to provide encouragement, challenge, and understanding can be of great value, especially to the junior and senior high school gifted student.

learning disabled

The learning disabled ("L.D.") student may be one of low mental ability, or a student of average ability who has some specific problems that prevent him or her from learning as rapidly or easily as others. Each problem will need to be considered, if you are to meet individual needs. It is important to consult with parents to find out what the child is able to do and likes to do.

Your first choice in planning should be to develop as many activities as you can that involve manipulatives. Puzzles, puppets, paper figures, or other objects to handle will enhance their learning.

Your second choice of effective techniques for teaching the learning disabled child will be a visual approach. Use pictures, charts, graphs, filmstrips, etc. that are appropriate to the child's ability and your lesson. When you talk, try to combine your words with either visual aids or tactile materials.

The child who is extremely disabled mentally may need a one-on-one approach. The child with a low mental age (regardless of actual age) will benefit from an in-the-room tutor. Try to enlist a mature teenager or adult who will volunteer to provide this special help. This helper should not be looked upon as one who is present only for the purpose of disciplining the student but as a "special friend" who will assist the student with activities. Other students in the class will learn quickly from this example and develop an understanding, helping attitude toward the less able student.

When it is not possible to secure a tutor, these suggestions may work:
1. Sit the child near the teacher so it is easy to supply needed assistance.
2. Assign more advanced students to assist the child with various activities throughout the day.
3. Provide a quiet corner, table, or carrel where the disabled child can work with less distraction.
4. Endeavor to secure volunteers for portions of each day for specific learning activities.

handicapped students

Consideration must be given for handicapped children, depending on their need. As previously mentioned, the hearing-impaired student should be seated where he or she can best hear and see the teacher. Many hearing impaired use facial expressions and a degree of lip reading for extra help in hearing, so it is important for them to see the face of the speaker. The student with a vision problem will also need to be seated in the best location to see the board or other visual materials. Glare from windows may be a problem for those who have difficulty seeing. The teacher will want to be aware of special needs of students in wheelchairs, on crutches, or with other physical problems. Observe and be sensitive to their needs, as well as taking time to secure helpful information from parents.

Effective Activities

. . . learning centers

Whether called learning stations, learning centers, study centers, activity areas, or any one of a number of other names, when properly executed, these activities can be valuable assets in your efforts to individualize in your classroom.

> ▶ *food for thought*
>
> If you don't trust children, forget about learning centers.

their purpose

A true learning center is much more than an amusement area, play corner, or display table. It is a location set aside where a child, or a small group of children, can learn about a particular topic. An effort is made to make the study highly motivating through the use of attractive displays, unusual materials, or different types of student involvement. The learning center is designed to foster independent learning, but carefully structured instructions must be given. Keep in mind that self-motivated children are rare—the teacher will always be the prime motivating force. Something catchy and new may start them off, but organization and scheduling (planned by the teacher) will keep them going!

The child must understand clearly what he or she is expected to do, in a step-by-step procedure, but the outcome may be uniquely his or her own.

The purpose of the learning center may be to teach something new or to reinforce or enrich a skill or concept. The materials and activities, of course, must be within the range of abilities and interests of the class.

Learning centers are not the only way to individualize instruction, but they are often an excellent way to begin meeting individual needs. They can become vehicles for moving children away from a completely teacher centered learning situation into worthwhile independent activities. The use of learning centers helps the teacher to organize and plan effective instruction for each individual child, providing each with a degree of freedom, movement, and choice while following a structured learning pattern.

These additional purposes for the learning center should be considered:
- to develop activities for meeting individual needs
- to develop independent learning habits and research skills
- to provide enjoyable, different activities
- to allow children to move about, working in different areas of the room
- to free the teacher to work with small groups or individuals
- to allow for group discussions where children can freely express their opinions.

organizational patterns

Free choice—The student signs up in advance to use the center at a specific time. This choice is whether or not to go to the learning center. Another free choice may be the selection between several centers in the room.

Assignment—The assignment to a learning center is good for reluctant learners or the shy and fearful. It is sometimes helpful to assign a friend to work with them to give them confidence. Assignment is also a good technique to use with students who have special learning problems.

Rotation system—The five in five system is good as a starter, if you meet five days a week. Have one center—five groups—one group each day at the center for five days. If you meet once weekly, start with one center—four groups—one group at the center each week for four weeks. In this system, children will not decide when to work at a center but may decide what they will work on while at the center.

Contracting—In this system, student and teacher discuss and agree on work to be done relating to a specific center. Work may be done at the center, at home, in the library, etc. This is best for more capable students, as greater ability in decision-making is involved.

Combination—must and may—musts at this center are determined by the teacher, based on specific needs of the student(s). *Mays* are choices given the students as to when they will go to the center, or a choice of activities at the center which are optional.

Hint: Don't make the "mays" a reward for all work done. Some children will never get to make a choice under this system. Every child needs a chance to make choices once in a while.

how to use them

Start simply! Don't try to begin with six learning centers around your room and turn the children loose. This plan will be doomed to chaos and failure unless you have a very unusual class and nerves of steel! Keep in mind these four words:

PREPARE   INTRODUCE   MOTIVATE   RECORD

1. *Prepare all aspects of the learning center.* Decide what you wish for the children to learn. Decide what type of activity will help them learn. Decide what materials will be needed. Decide what will be done with the finished work. Decide how you will record each child's participation at the center. Use a checklist to be sure you have included all the needed items.

A good learning center might have:

something to do: games
dittos
task cards
puzzles
records or tapes to hear

something to make: pictures
diagrams
mobiles
models

something to see: filmstrips
pictures
nature objects
collections (missionary items, etc.)

Most learning centers will have not just one, but a combination of these activities. You might like to begin with a general interest center such as a missionary center. It might include:
- a taped message from the missionary (or the missionary's children)
- pictures of the mission
- a ditto map to mark or fill in some way (varied with age and ability of group).

Many teachers like to follow the learning center format of:
- something to see
- something to touch
- something to hear
- something to do and keep.

2. *Introduce your learning center by establishing rules for its use.* Once the procedures are learned, the atmosphere is right for successful use of the center. When the children have learned to move from the whole group to the learning center activity in a relaxed, pleasant way, you are ready to try multiple learning centers. You and your class should decide on working rules together. Here are some "starters" made up by children:

- Help each other.
- Stay at the center until you finish the work.
- Have quiet conversations.
- Follow the directions carefully.
- Take turns with materials.
- Be careful with materials so as not to waste.
- Leave everything nice for the next people.

Notice how the teacher carefully helped the children phrase each rule in a positive "do" way rather than a negative "don't" manner.

3. *Motivate your class to a keen interest in the learning center through imaginative planning.* Several centers planned around a central theme will be more interesting than several unrelated centers. A pocket chart is an excellent way to develop a learning center's theme, motivate choices, and keep a record of each child's activities.

Each child selects a card from the colored pocket. He writes his name on the card and checks his name off when he completes the activity. The center may be identified by a colored poster of the same color as the pocket so younger children can easily find it.

44

Centers are fun to create, and once you start you will find that many ideas for developing them will come to you. The Holy Land Trip pocket chart illustrates a way of organizing several centers around a central theme. Seasonal themes can be equally effective and are easy to develop. Here is a listing of ideas to help you get started:

- Bible quiz
- Bible game
- discussion topic (story with a moral)
- Bible map center
- listening center (Bible story, character-building story)
- creating center (greeting cards, writing stories)
- filmstrip center (Bible stories)
- music center (a hymn with a related story to read)
- art center (great religious art)
- church membership center (what does it mean? etc.)
- "our church" center
- reading center (Bible story with activities)
- poetry center (read or create)
- viewing center (slides of the Holy Land)
- church news center (read the church paper)
- thinking center (open-ended story)
- mission center
- what is a deacon? elder? etc. center

4. *Record the participation of the children in learning centers.* There are several good reasons for record keeping. First, the success of your learning center can usually be measured by the number of children who successfully complete the activity. If it has a poor record, you will probably want to revise the activities before using the idea another time. Second, children like to know *you care* about what they are doing. If you keep a record, they have a reason for telling you when a task is done. They want you to know, and it means more if you mark it down in some way. Something *finished* is progress for the child, and that's important. Some teachers like to recognize this progress by reporting it to parents from time to time. You will find ideas on this in the last chapter. Third, record keeping helps prevent confusion as to who is working at which center. Sometimes activities cannot be completed in one day, so a simple check mark on a card can help us out where our memories may fail!

▶ *food for thought*

Take your learning center down one day (or week) before it dies.

when to use them

Learning centers are seldom used as the total instructional program. Some teachers like to use them instead of the more traditional "activity" or "workbook" time, incorporating these parts of the lessons into the learning centers. Other teachers effectively use learning centers during an "extended" or second session if they have their class during both Bible school and church. In some cases, a learning center might better suit the needs of a particular student or students. In this situation, the teacher would excuse these students from the group as a whole to work at the center. The answer to "when?" is "any time it suits you best!"

... learning center examples

SOUNDS IN GOD'S WORLD CENTER

Record a series of sounds on a cassette. Leave a space between each sound of about five seconds. Some of the sounds you could record might be:

wind	dog barking	rain on a roof
someone humming	cat's meow	or window
street sounds	horn honking	door slamming

Five sounds will be enough to put on your tape. If you can secure headsets and a multiple outlet listening unit, this equipment is nice for a small group to use, while others are involved elsewhere. If not, put the group in a far corner with the tape turned low.

Needed: cassette recorder, tape, paper, and pencil

Recommended age: Beginner through junior high

RECORD A MESSAGE CENTER

Try to arrange a quiet corner or converted closet for a taping center area. Have students sign up in advance. Decide on a time limit. Students may use your suggestions or decide on a message of their own. Play the tapes for the class, one or two at a time, at the end of the day. (Suggestion: Listen to the tapes before playing them for the class.)

Needed: cassette recorder, tape, mike

Recommended age: Grade 4 through junior high

LOOKING GLASS CENTER

Have a mirror and directions at the center. When you look at yourself, what do you see? If you look closely you may see—a picture? a story? Write a story or draw a picture of what you see.

Needed: mirror, directions, paper, pencils, and crayons or colored pencils

Recommended age: Grades 3-5

GIVE ADVICE CENTER

Prepare a number of three by five-inch cards with brief appropriate problems. Ask students to read the cards and answer the questions. They may put their answers in a pocket at the learning center.

Needed: question cards, paper, and pencils

Recommended age: Grades 4-7

I AM A MOTHER. I HAVE A LITTLE GIRL. SHE IS NAUGHTY AT BEDTIME. WHAT SHOULD I DO?

ANSWER SHEET

BIBLE DETECTIVE

Decorate a large piece of poster board as shown. Use sentences appropriate to your class. Laminate the poster with clear contact paper. Let students write source with grease pencil. Glue a check sheet to the back of the poster, or put it in an envelope on the lower front corner.

Variation: Give students the Scripture sources in advance. Let them match the sources with the statements. Encourage the use of the Bible to look up the Scriptures to be certain of getting the correct source.

Needed: poster, grease pencil, and Bible

Recommended age: Grades 4-8

SHAPE-BOOK CENTER

Make up a number of shaped booklets by cutting out the desired shape on a fold. Let students select the booklet they desire, writing the appropriate words inside. Suggestions for starters:

Love is . . .

A helping hand is . . .

Bad is . . .

Good is . . .

The Bible says . . .

Needed: booklets, Bible for reference, and pencils

Recommended age: Grades 2-4

INDIVIDUALIZED BIBLE READING

Each child should have a pocket for his/her card. Every week each child records what has been read in the Bible on the card. Every week, for two or three minutes, the class teacher should discuss alone with the child his/her reading. It is important to answer questions, discuss difficult words, and encourage the child. Praise good work and listen to individual comments.

Needed: poster board, envelopes, 3″ x 5″ cards, pencil, marker or pictures to decorate poster

Recommended age: Grades 4-8

BIBLE BASKET OR
TRAVELING SUITCASE

Beginner and Primary children love to take something home. Either a basket or small suitcase can be used for this "homework" activity. Decorate the basket or suitcase. Fill with religious books, a Bible, records, puzzle, crayons, and a picture to color and return. Be sure to include a letter to parents with directions for use. Tell which items should be returned (if any) and which may be used by the child and kept. Let the parent know when it should be returned. Children will love this and look forward to their turn.

Needed: basket or small suitcase, appropriate items to fill

Recommended age: Preschool—Grade 2

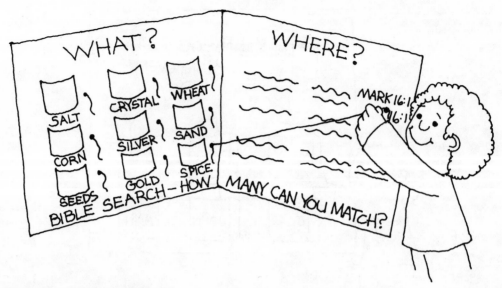

BIBLE SEARCH CENTER

Staple various small elements or items in plastic bags. Attach these to a board. Print the Scripture where the item is named on the opposite side. Attach yarn near the element and use it to match with the Scripture. Yarn may be wrapped around a paper fastener.

Needed: cardboard, plastic bags, elements, Bible dictionary, yarn, paper fasteners, magic marker

Recommended age: Grade 4 through junior high

MINI-CREATURE CENTER

Older children will enjoy contributing to this center once they have seen an example. It is important to guide the children in their observations of these small creatures. Draw their attention to specific features, give them Biblical references, or secure a few books about insects to place on the table.

The "Creature Cage" is made with a half gallon or gallon cardboard milk carton. Cut an opening in one side. Pull a sheer hose over the carton. Reach inside and put your "creature" in the cage. Tie securely at each end. Pull the tie at the bottom around to the back if you wish to rest the cage on a table. Hang on a hook or a string from the ceiling, if you wish. Just keep the creatures for one lesson and let them go so they will not die for lack of food and water.

Needed: milk cartons, nylon hose, yarn or string

Recommended age: Preschool through grade 6

50

LET YOUR FINGERS DO THE WALKING (through the Bible . . .)

Design a large, laminated poster as shown. Give a Bible fact and three sources after it. Students circle (if laminated) or write on paper (if not laminated) the correct source. "Walk" fingers through the Bible to be sure of correct source.

Needed: poster, Bible, paper, pencils, and grease pencil
Recommended age: Grades 4-8

GOOD FEELING CENTER

Put one child's picture or name on an attractive poster in the center. Provide paper with uniform-spaced punched holes at the center. During the session each child, except the one pictured, goes to the center and writes something he *likes* about the person who is featured. At the end of the class, after a quick check, the teacher puts the picture of the child on a cover and fastens all papers into a booklet. Arrange for each child to take home a "Good Feelings" booklet during the quarter. The teacher should be sure to add his or her comment to the booklet, too.

Emphasize that good feelings expressed to others are one of the ways we show our love. Tell the children to watch for the things they like about others so they'll be ready to write something when that person's picture appears. This is an excellent way to encourage *positive* thoughts about others.

Needed: booklet cover, paper, and pencils
Recommended age: Grades 4-7

PUT-IT-ALL TOGETHER (small group activity)

Divide a recent lesson story into several parts. Write or type each part on a card. Mix up the cards and put them at the learning center. Appoint a leader for the activity. Let the group go to the center.

The leader reads the first part of the story which has been given to him in advance. Each other member of the group then takes a card. Pupils work together to put the story in order. When all agree on the order, they signal the teacher (or at the end of the class, they may report). They stand in a line in order, each person reading his part of the story to the class.

Variation: If your class is small, this can be a whole class activity.

Needed: story cards

Recommended age: Grades 3-6

STORY GO-TOGETHERS

This is an activity that can be done with younger children since no reading is required. It can be done alone, but some children will enjoy doing it with a partner. The purpose of this activity is to help young children to become familiar with Bible stories, so it is a helpful way to review stories already taught. Do not put more than three to five pairs in one envelope. Cut and mount matching pictures from Bible stories you have told. Laminate them. Put three to five pairs in a decorated envelope. Let the children match up the pairs.

Needed: 9″ x 12″ brown envelope, small pictures (2 for each story), clear contact paper for laminating pictures

Recommended age: Preschool—Grade 2

"WHAT IS IT?" CENTER

Can you guess what is in the bag? Feel it. Write about it. *Possible items:* very small Bible, plastic praying hands, plastic cross, book marker, paper clip.

Needed: bag and object, pencils, and paper

Recommended age: 3-7

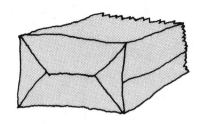

GOD WAS...
Happy 😊   Sad 😟

Matthew 3:1	Genesis 6:6

DIRECTIONS
1. You have 15 minutes.
2. Try to find 5 examples for each column.
3. Give teacher your paper.

HOW DID GOD FEEL?

Several students at a time can work at this activity. The poster at the center is mainly to motivate students and help them get started. Be sure to have a time limit and tell students what to do with their completed work.

Needed: Bibles, concordance, Bible dictionary, paper, pencil, poster board, magic marker

Recommended age: Grades 4-8

WHICH WORD DISAGREES (small group activity—teacher led)

This is a good activity for younger (ages 4-8) children to encourage good listening habits. Use your lesson story papers.

The teacher holds up the picture. He says four or five words, all *but one* which would be logically associated with the picture. One word obviously does not fit. Children are asked to listen for the word that does not fit. After all the words are said, ask children to tell which one did not fit.

Example: picture—Jesus and the children

words—children, Jesus, love, game, come

word that does not fit—game

Needed: pictures and word choices

Recommended age: Grades 1-4

. . . keeping records

Every learning center should have a record (such as the following example) that the teacher keeps. It will help you in two ways. First, it will help you be sure to have clear objectives, methods, and materials on hand. It will also help you to know how many children are using the activity and to record and evaluate its successes or failures. Second, such forms can be kept in a central resource file to provide an excellent source of ideas for all of the teachers in your school. File the ideas by age or department and then cross file them by topic.

LEARNING CENTER TOPIC:_____

SUGGESTED AGE: _____

OBJECTIVES:

1. _____

2. _____

3. _____

4. _____

METHOD: (Describe briefly)

MATERIALS NEEDED:

1. By teacher, to make the center:

2. By pupils, to use the center:

PUPILS AT CENTER AT ONE TIME _____

EVALUATION:

1. Pupil reaction:

_____ Excellent _____ Good _____ Fair _____ Poor

2. Objectives met:

_____ All pupils _____ Some _____ Few _____ None

SUGGESTIONS FOR REVISIONS:

_____ File for future use   _____ Do not file

_____ Developer of Center
                    (name)

. . . ten ideas to try

Successful teaching includes many different types of activities. The effective teacher collects ideas, using them when they are most appropriate for the interests and needs of her current students. Following are ten ideas of various types that may be "starters" for your collection:

1. SCRIPTURE CHORAL SPEAKING

Teachers have used choral reading for many years. However, choral *speaking* is different because the passages are memorized. This makes it especially appropriate for use in religious education. Scripture passages memorized become a source of lifelong strength and inspiration. Added motivation for memorization is provided when it is to be used with a group of friends in a choral speaking presentation.

Teaching Tips:

- Older students should write verses to be memorized.
- Set a deadline for memorization.
- Ask students to say or read the verses at least once daily. Short, frequent repetition aids in memorization.
- Assign solo parts after all have memorized verses.
- Plan a performance to give students a goal.
- When performing, alternate between boys and girls, or high and low pitched voices, to give variety.
- Use occasional solos.
- Alternate dynamics—even try a whisper if it suits the verses.

Points to tell your students:

- They will be a choir that speaks instead of sings.
- Sometimes they will all speak together, and at times there will be solos, duets, or trios, just like in a singing choir.
- They should practice at home saying the Scripture slowly, clearly, and with expression.
- They will need to work hard to stay together, all talking at the same speed and pitch.

This idea, presented with enthusiasm and a performance goal, is a highly motivating one for students from grade 4 all the way through high school.

2. ONE DAY MIRACLE MURAL

This is a great activity to get students working together and give them a feeling of accomplishment.

Needed: Mural paper (about three feet per team), chalk, crayons, or (if you are brave) poster paint

Procedure:

1. Divide your class into teams, three on a team.

2. Instruct each team to select one of Jesus' miracles. Provide Scripture references, if needed.
3. Assign each team one section of the mural paper.
4. Each team will depict their miracle in one of these two ways:
   - Color the background. Then draw figures on separate paper, cut out, and glue on the background. Print a title and Scripture reference at the bottom.
   - Color the background. Sketch figures in black crayon outlines first, then complete the coloring of them, coloring over background.

It is best, in this one-day project, to have students color in entire background area first. This avoids the tedious task of coloring around small areas in the figures. Take the mural to a hall area where it can be seen by all!

3. BIBLE-SCHOOL NEWSPAPER

Juniors and older students will get excited about this activity. High school students may enjoy such a project on a regular basis—monthly or quarterly.

How to proceed:
1. Decide on topics to be included, such as:
   - Class news—statistics, teachers' names, interesting activities, etc.
   - Features about people—unusual items, awards, visitors, etc.
   - Interviews—minister, superintendent, organist, choir director, etc.
   - Dear Abby—letters and answers
   - Cartoons
   - Coming events
2. Appoint an editor.
3. Ask for volunteer reporters to complete the selected topics.
4. Allow the students time to gather information. They may need to phone for appointments. It is a good idea to make special name tags for stu-

dent identification if they are to be in various parts of the school building.

5. Give a specific time when articles are due. The editor should help edit and correct articles.

6. Enlist a parent to help type the paper on ditto stencils.

If you discuss the project with your school office staff before you start, you may be able to secure their help with the duplication of your paper. Give them plenty of time.

If you cannot get your paper duplicated, mount all the articles on mural paper under an appropriate heading. Display it in the hall or on your classroom door. It will create a lot of interest!

4. INSTANT PLAY

Select a simple Bible story with several characters. Read it to the class. List the characters on the board or chart paper. Decide on the number of scenes and where the "stage" will be in the room.

For the first presentation, select volunteers who are the most capable and outgoing. This will encourage others. No rehearsal is needed. The dialogue and acting should be spontaneous.

When it is over, ask students to evaluate. Which characters did the best job? Why? What would improve the play? Discuss facial expression, body movement, voice quality, diction, and dialogue.

Select a second cast to do the same play again. This activity will help students learn to work together, develop speaking ability, and make Bible stories more meaningful.

5. PAPER BAG PUPPET STORY

Select a Bible story with good action and several interesting characters (for example, Daniel in the lions' den).

If you have a large class, divide the class into several groups with three or four children in each group. Each group may select its own story.

Use small, lunch size paper bags. Draw the face on the bottom of the bag (see sample). Color the lower part of the bag appropriately.

Students can get behind a table, screen, or chart rack, holding characters up over the edge to tell the stories.

Hand puppets are excellent for younger children and often help to "bring out" the shy child.

6. BIBLE FASHION SHOW

Bring some books to class on Biblical dress, or have a collection of old Bible-school papers, so students can look through them and decide on authentic costumes. Discuss the colors available in the period of history of the costume and the kinds of material people used. Discuss the various kinds of dress—tax collector, soldiers, shepherds, wife of an innkeeper, city woman, etc. Use long sheets of brown or white mural paper (or table covering). Have a partner trace the child's basic body shape lightly in pencil. Include the headdress as a part of the costume. Draw the entire costume to cover the body shape and color it appropriately.

Cut a hole for the head *after* the headdress and balance of the costume are drawn and colored. Draw arms to the front and cut a hole for hands and lower arm to come through and hold costume in place. Cut out entire costume.

Present a fashion show for another class, or invite parents to come and see it!

If you have the wall space, when finished, tape costumes to the wall for decoration.

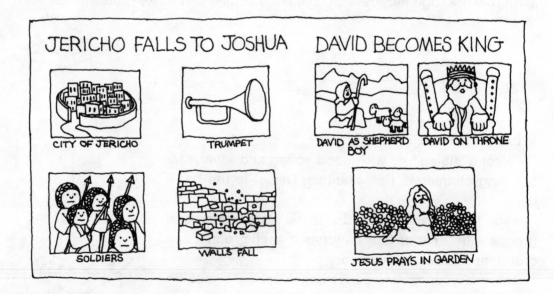

7. HEADLINER MURAL

This is an excellent use of your old collection of pictures. During one class session have the students decide on imaginative, modern-day "headlines" for each picture. If you have several pictures for one story, these can all be grouped under one headline. Use a piece of mural paper and print headlines in bold, block print with wide magic marker. Make them big—at least three inch letters. At the end of the first class session, collect all pictures.

In the second session, divide the class into small groups of three. Give each group several pictures. Put the mural "headliner" on the wall or bulletin board. Let students glue the pictures under the correct headline. If there are several pictures for a headline, they may print a subhead under each picture.

This is an excellent way to review a series of lessons!

8. SORTING OUT PROPAGANDA

Use six small cans with plastic lids. Cut slits in the lids and decorate the cans with contact paper. Label cans. Discuss and explain the following definitions at a whole group session so students will be certain to understand them:

LABEL	EXPLANATION
Testimonial	A well-known person testifies that he or she has used a product (drugs, drink, etc.) or supports a cause. ("Do away with all rules.")
Transfer	The statement suggests a transfer of certain qualities of a well-known person to a product. ("*Name* uses drug. You should try it.")

Glittering Generalities	The statement makes a sweeping, unsupported statement about a cause or product. ("It's the most marvelous feeling you've ever had!" or "It will be the greatest party you have ever attended!")
Name Calling	The statement uses emotional words to affect people's attitudes in the absence of facts. ("*Name* wouldn't try it. He's a dimwit.")
The Bandwagon	The statement endeavors to persuade by such statements as "Everybody's doing it!" or "The whole school likes it."
Card Stacking	The statement presents a case for a cause or product, but care is taken to present only favorable information. ("You should try smoking. *You* don't know anybody who has gotten lung cancer from smoking." or "The new cigarettes have effective filters." or "Some research has said it isn't harmful.")

This activity can be initiated with a few statements by the teacher, but is most effective when students begin to watch for statements and add them to the list. Statements are written on cards and sorted into the correct container. A key should be provided. Number each card when added, and the number key, so checking is quick and easy. This can be an individual activity or easily adapted into a game. This activity is best for junior high youth departments when peer pressures become a problem.

9. FACT OR OPINION

Prepare cards with a Bible "truth" or "opinion." On the back side put the correct answer. If the card is a fact, give the Scripture reference to encourage reliance on the Bible for truth. Put cards (statement side up) in the center of a large piece of colored poster board on which you have drawn a pathway, divided into squares. A small religious article can be used for a marker.

1. Spin a spinner or roll a number cube for points.
2. Draw. Give answer ("fact" or "opinion"). If correct, move marker the number of points spun or rolled.
3. The first player to reach the end (a church, a heavenly crown, etc., may be used at the end) wins.

For longer wear, laminate board, spinner, and cards. Here are some sample statements:

Opinion: "Churches should not use hymnbooks."

Fact: "Baptism was commanded by Christ" (Matthew 28:19).

10. SHAKE, RATTLE, AND READ!

Decorate the top of an egg carton with the name of the game. Mark the name of a different book of the Bible on each egg carton. These are easy to make, so why not make several?

On the inside, use magic marker and number each space from one to twelve.

Put two or three buttons, beans, or small stones in each carton. If you want an extra quiet game, use small pieces of cotton, rolled tightly, or little squares of sponge.

After the student shakes, he opens the carton and decides how to arrange the numbers to make his Scripture reference. Example: For the illustration shown, you might read:

Matthew 1:9-11, Matthew 9:1-11, or Matthew 11:1-9.

▶ *food for thought*

For the spirit to live its freest, the mind must acknowledge discipline.

. . . Sylvia Ashton-Warner*

*Warner, Sylvia Ashton. *Teacher,* Simon and Schuster, Inc., 1963.

5

Effective Discipline

... classroom management and control

Why is it that some teachers seldom appear to have discipline problems and others consistently have classes that are in turmoil? Numerous studies have been undertaken to answer this question. Sometimes teachers who are sincere in their desire to help students learn are plagued by classroom problems. They know what they want students to do, but never seem quite able to accomplish their goals.

Considerations of discipline fall into two categories. The first, broad area is that of general classroom management and control. This involves the techniques used by the teacher to achieve some kind of control of the entire class. The second consideration is that involving reasons for and solutions to individual problems. Of course, the two are closely related. It is recognized that there is no real group solution to individual problems. However, there are techniques a teacher can use to "get the class under control," just as there are times when individual students may be disruptive when the class as a whole is well managed.

Students who are not identified as having individual problems may become involved in general classroom disorder. The teacher in this situation may not know where to start to solve the problem on an individual basis, because it appears that every student is involved. In such a situation some common disciplinary errors may occur.

... seven frequent errors

1. Using grades or reports to control
2. Giving learning activities as punishment
3. Intentionally causing fear, tension, or anxiety
4. Punishing the whole class because of a few
5. Physical or verbal abuse
6. Making promises
7. Ignoring a student for long periods

using grades to control

Perhaps you do not give letter or number grades, unless you are a teacher in a Christian day school. However, all teachers should avoid sending letters to the parents of every child to report poor class behavior. This is, in effect, a blanket report on conduct. Conduct reports should concern individuals, not groups. There is little a parent can do to control a teacher's class. If you are specific, and give individual reports, the parent may be able to assist by discussions at home. "They didn't learn what they should have, because the whole class was so bad," is a type of learning evaluation that indicates the teacher, as well as the students, has failed to carry out responsibilities. It must be remembered that the teacher is ultimately responsible for control of the class so that learning can take place.

giving learning activities as punishment

This practice creates negative attitudes toward the learning goals you wish to accomplish. If learning is used for punishment, you can expect that it will be difficult to convince students that learning can be exciting, pleasant, and worthwhile. Such practices as writing words repetitiously, writing sentences, writing Scriptures, writing math facts, etc., fall into this category.

intentionally using fear or anxiety

Threats of any kind are a misuse of discipline. Threats creating fear or anxiety may include such statements as:

"God knows what you are doing and He will punish you."

"If you don't behave the devil will get you."

"You'll never get to Heaven if you act like that."

Young children are inclined to take such statements literally and can become fearful to the extent of having nightmares or refusing to go to church if such threats are frequent.

punishment of the whole class

Of all areas of misuse of discipline, this may be the most frequently used. This is true in spite of the fact that most teachers realize this is an unjust technique. Usually such punishment evolves from teacher desperation. He or she is unable to find the culprit, or pinpoint one or two trouble-makers. It may *seem* that the whole class is misbehaving! Denial of special privileges, treats, or a part of the learning program are examples of this type of disciplinary technique.

physical or verbal abuse

Physical abuse is usually easy to identify. Slapping children, yanking too forcefully, pushing too hard, slamming down into a chair are all actions unworthy of any teacher. It is more difficult to discern verbal abuse, and often the teacher using it is not aware of the crushing effect it has on a child. Obvious examples are name-calling or sarcasm. Less obvious are insinuations—"I don't know *why* you can't get that," or "This *ought* to be easy enough for you." If such comments are a part of the teacher's routine, students soon refuse to try rather than risk the danger of ridicule, sarcasm, or shame.

▶ *food for thought*

The value one sees in himself must come partly from the value others place upon him.

making promises

Promises, like threats, are usually made by the teacher out of despair when there is a loss of control or when she cannot think of anything else to do. Extra playtime, a cookie treat, or a "surprise," may be promised if the children are good. Threats and promises may appear to be easy solutions to class problems, but they can be a sure way to future trouble. Alternating between the two tends to confuse students and both techniques create similar pressures. Too frequently used, threats and promises of reward become meaningless rather than legitimate methods for motivating students. They offer only the postponement of a problem, rather than a solution.

ignoring pupils for long periods

The disruptive child is difficult to ignore in the classroom. However, it is important not to remove this child from the class so often, or for so long, that chances of improvement within the group are slim. It will be difficult for the disruptive child to learn to control his or her behavior in the classroom if seldom a part of the group. If well planned and used effectively, temporary removal from the group can be a valid technique. Our ultimate goal, however, should be to assist the child in making changes in behavior so work can be done effectively within the group. Removal from the group should give the child a chance to bring himself or herself under control and successfully reenter the group.

What then *are* the solutions to general classroom management problems? There are many, and no guarantees exist that any *one* will work for any single classroom. The teacher must have the ability to step back and look at the situation in an objective way and be willing to try different methods. Reflecting on his studies, Robert Di Guilio (Di Guilio, Robert. "The Guaranteed Behavior Improvement Plan." *Teacher,* April, 1978, pp. 22-26) maintains that there is only *one* unchangeable, "carved in stone" precept influencing pupil behavior. He insists, "The vast majority of discipline problems are caused directly or indirectly by the teacher." Nothing could be more blunt, or more true. It is time for teachers to recognize that they cannot blame all discipline problems on the home, the combination of children in the class, the genes, or other external factors. *Teachers* are themselves many times responsible! The teacher who has few discipline problems is clearly in control because:

- she knows what she wishes to accomplish
- she has everything ready to do it
- she knows how to make changes to meet the needs of the student.

Good class management requires a teacher who is firm but polite, treating students with the same dignity and courtesy given to adults. Just as she would never tell an adult to "shut up," neither would she ever say that to a child. Respecting children as worthy recipients of kind, considerate treatment must be the goal of the effective Christian teacher.

▶ *food for thought*

If you have a child who never wants to be working in his seat, try this: set a timer at random short spans of time. If he's in his seat working when it rings, reward him. Increase the span of time for gradually longer periods.

... problems with individuals

If problems are occurring frequently with several students in a group, the first consideration must be whether or not the rules are fair, acceptable, and understood. Be sure rules have been discussed, agreed upon to be reasonable, and consequences explained. If this has been done, the following steps for dealing with individual problems may be followed:

1. Talk to the child privately, explaining the misbehavior. If rules are posted on a chart and have been reviewed, this need not be defended by the teacher. Criticize the poor *behavior,* not the child. Make it very clear that this is a rule that all the students have agreed upon. Be firm in your commitment and insist on the child following the rules for the good of the entire group.

2. If the behavior is extreme or disruptive to the progress of the lesson, remove the child from the group quickly and firmly with little or no comment. A chair behind a screen or outside the classroom door will serve as a "cooling off place." Comment firmly, "Please sit here until I have a free minute so we can talk this over."
If the problem is less serious just change the child's seat, or move to sit beside him, again without undue comment.

3. Have the follow-up discussion with the child as soon as you can. In this discussion, talk about how the behavior should be changed, rather than "why" it happened. Insist that the child tell you, in his own words, what rule was broken and how he can correct the problem. Children usually cannot tell you why a misbehavior happened without blaming someone else. This is normal. If the child is intent on the idea that someone else is responsible for his problem, a "change request" (see Example 1 at the end of this section) may be helpful. This has proven effective because it focuses thought on something positive about the other person and how the misbehaving child can *help* the other person to change.

4. If the behavior has been repeated and the above techniques have brought no change, a Behavior Modification Contract might be effective (see Examples 2, 3, and 4). Again the child should state, in his own words, the rules that must be followed. The contract adds the consequences that will be adhered to by the teacher if the rule is broken again. If the child is young, or has difficulty writing, the teacher should fill in the contract as the child dictates. Ask the child to sign the contract, however.

5. Consequences may include:

- a letter or call to parent from teacher
- be very specific describing the exact behavior, giving the rule broken and avoiding emotional terms or evaluations as to why the problem is occurring.
- invite the parent to come to discuss the problem. Avoid lengthy "counseling sessions." This is not the teacher's role. Try to get information from the parent and work with the parent to decide what future action will be taken. It is appropriate to ask the parent to take some specific responsibility. This might include observing the class session or securing counseling for the child and family. Seek a mutual understanding as to how you can work together to assist the child in learning acceptable behavior.

6. Be sure the child has class work he is capable of doing. Many discipline problems occur when the child is unable to do assignments. Review techniques for meeting individual needs, and make sure you are well acquainted with the needs of this particular child. Are there physical problems? Where is he in his intellectual development? What are his social needs? Be professional, be thorough.

▶ *food for thought*

When a good student helps a poor student, *both* students improve in knowledge and skills.

7. Try to give the child positive recognition *when he does something deserving.* Give him small responsibilities he can complete and praise him when they are well done. Caution: Avoid comments that give mixed messages such as, "Why can't you do that all the time?" The compliment is negated by the reminder that the teacher is remembering past faults. It is important to base compliments or rewards on good work or behavior, not on sympathy for the child.

8. Determine at what time or under what circumstances the child is most disruptive. Is it during work assignments, when lining up, during breaks, or recess? Is it near the end of the morning when he is tired or hungry? These considerations will give clues as to possible solutions.

9. Consider disciplinary alternatives you have not tried. Remember that not every method is successful with every child. Study the list below for ideas you may not have considered:

discipline alternatives

- Please stop it
- Add responsibilities
- Humor (not sarcasm)
- Sit with me
- Sit with . . .
- Think time
- Stop watch—work for . . . minutes
- Ticket for . . . (earned by good behavior)
- Nonverbal reminder (facial or body movement)
- Parent involvement—helpers in class
- Supervisor involvement (department chairman, minister, etc.)
- Nothing contract (do "nothing" for a definite period of time)
- Quiet time out
- Listen to music
- Private talks
- Isolation for a short time
- Withdraw privileges
- Ignore the behavior
- Positive reinforcement when good
- Act out the misbehavior
- Act out desired behavior
- Group problem-solving discussion
- Make responsibility charts
- Behavior contract
- Legitimize the behavior
- *You* teach for five minutes
- Change the environment
- Suspend from the class for a stated period of time
- Silence
- Request more help
- Secure an advocate

. . . suggestions for working with four types of problem students

A. THE DISINTERESTED OR WITHDRAWN STUDENT

This student, while not disrupting the class, is often discouraging to the teacher. He does not take part willingly and is a cause for concern because he is not realizing his full potential.

1. Praise whenever it is possible to do so. "I appreciate how quietly Jane is listening," may seem to be reinforcing the very behavior you would like to change, but it will help put the student at ease and give him confidence.
2. Assign a partner to help involve the student.
3. Begin with very short activities, gradually increasing their difficulty and duration.
4. Learn all you can about the interests and hobbies of the student and incorporate these into his assignments or into your class discussions.

B. THE NEGATIVE STUDENT

This may be a student who is with you at the insistence of a parent or older brother or sister. He may have a very sullen or antagonistic outlook. Criticism of others or class activities is frequent. He may refuse to do assignments or fail to complete them.
1. Concentrate on and praise whatever cooperative behavior you observe.
2. Break work into small tasks, making sure it is not too difficult and can be quickly completed.
3. Be sure that consequences for poor behavior are clear and predictable.
4. Ignore in a casual way criticisms of the student. Don't let him get under your skin. Give him an example of courtesy and affectionate concern.
5. Be prepared to modify tasks and change assignments if the student becomes negative but will accept a reasonable alternate assignment.

C. THE IMPULSIVE STUDENT

This student is often in trouble because he has not learned self-control. Help him to learn by following these suggestions:
1. Decrease permissiveness and give few choices.
2. Be sure the student knows exactly what is expected in behavior and in work assignments.
3. Give specific time limits.
4. Maintain a calm, organized atmosphere.
5. Use vivid colors and room decorations sparingly. This student is easily overstimulated by both sound and visuals.
6. Provide a student advocate.

D. THE ANXIOUS STUDENT

Fear is the companion of this student. He may decide in advance that the work will be too difficult for him or that he will not understand it. He may appear to be a "pest" because he asks for so much help, or frequently says, "Is this right?"
1. Give plenty of positive reinforcement when earned.
2. Be sure the student fully understands the task and support him when he is working with comments such as, "You're doing fine," "Keep up the good work," or "You're on the right track."

3. Reduce group competition—avoid situations that will put the student "on the spot" such as games or reading aloud.

4. Give small, easy assignments that will assure success, gradually increasing in difficulty.

summary

In the previous material you have read over and over again the need for teacher awareness of the student's individual abilities and interests. You have also noted that almost every type of behavior problem is "treated" with praise when earned, short, easy assignments to assure success, and a clear statement as to behavior expectations.

It is important for the teacher to remember that behavior problems usually will not go away if ignored. The causes and the solutions for misbehavior are developed over a long period of time. Research tells us that causes may be boredom, lack of interest, stress, poor group management, lack of trust, desire for attention, and/or poor self-concept. Discipline problems can be reduced by the teacher who has established clear, consistent boundaries, open communication, shared decision making, known consequences, many-optioned curriculum, and varied learning techniques.

▶ *food for thought*

Research shows that neatly written papers get more praise than less neat papers with the same answers. However, research has also found no correlation between handwriting and intelligence.

. . . discipline-related contracts, messages, and activities

Example 1

CHANGE REQUEST

DATE _____

FROM_____
                    (my name)

THE PERSON I WANT TO CHANGE IS:

_____

SOMETHING I *LIKE* ABOUT THIS PERSON IS:

_____

_____

_____

THE BEHAVIOR I WOULD LIKE TO CHANGE IS:

_____

_____

_____

I WILL HELP THIS PERSON TO CHANGE BY:

_____

_____

Example 2

BEHAVIOR MODIFICATION CONTRACT

RULES TO FOLLOW:

    1. _____

    2. _____

    3. _____

CONSEQUENCES:

    1. _____

    2. _____

    3. _____

SIGNED _____

                    Student

                  _____

                    Teacher

                  _____

                    Parent

DATE _____

Example 3

SAMPLE
CORRECTIVE
BEHAVIOR CONTRACT

_____   _____

               (name)   (date)

What: (Type of behavior about which we are concerned.)

How: (How we intend to work on our behavior.)

Length: (How long) From _____ to _____

Consequences: (What consequences do I accept?)

    1. _____

    2. _____

    3. _____

Beginning signatures   *Ending signatures*

_____   _____

student   student

_____   _____

teacher   teacher

_____   _____

parent   parent

Example 4

Dear _____

_____ is working on _____

_____

in Bible School. You can help at home by_____

_____

_____

_____ .

If you have any questions or comments please call me
(#_____ _____) or write them and return this sheet.

_____

_____

_____

Thank you very much for your time and help.

_____
Teacher

SPECIAL PERSON

AWARD

To_____

Our class has chosen
you the Special Person

this _____ day of _____

because _____

_____

_____

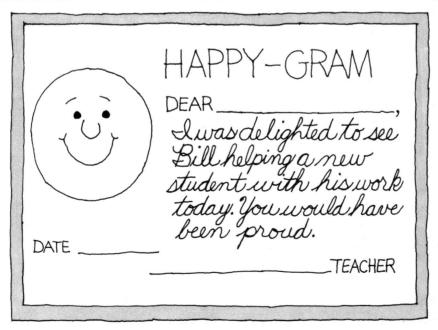

HAPPY-GRAM

DEAR_____,
I was delighted to see
Bill helping a new
student with his work
today. You would have
been proud.

DATE _____

_____TEACHER

Once in a while you *must* notify a parent of a less happy event. It might be done like this:

positive reinforcement

NON-COMPETITIVE REWARDS:
- *Warm fuzzies*
  special person award, letter from teacher, flower to wear, picture on bulletin board, special ribbon to wear, award certificate, etc.
- *Special jobs*
  something the student would like to do
- *Special responsibilities*
  passing out papers, feeding the turtle, etc.
- *Freedom of movement*
  taking attendance to the office, library pass, etc.
- *Helping others*
  help teach something to someone else
- *Care for others*
  give a warm fuzzy to another person
- *Doodle contract*
  free time when work is completed
- *Time line contract*
  student decides when work is to be completed
- *Freedom to select*
  student decides how he wants to learn

- *Food*

  ticket to go to the classroom refreshment stand

Group activities can be used to help children develop positive attitudes about themselves and others. Here are some examples:

STRANGER IN THE CLASS

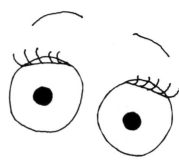

All eyes are on the person who interrupts your class. Plan ahead and make each interruption a learning experience.

Ask the class to look closely at each person who enters your room and decide on something they *like* about them. They will be eagerly awaiting the next visitor!

After the person leaves, let the students describe the person telling the things they liked. Make a list on the board or chart paper. For added "P.R." value, send the list to your visitor with a little note of explanation.

This activity develops visual skills as well as reinforcing the habit of a positive attitude toward others.

SHRINK OR SWELL?

This is an activity center lesson. Be sure to have all directions at the center. After students have had a few days to do the activity, remove the sentences and read them together. Use them as a basis for class discussion on how our comments can hurt or help others.

DIRECTIONS:

1. Write a sentence that would make someone "shrink."
2. Write a sentence that would make someone "swell."
3. Put your sentences in the correct envelope.

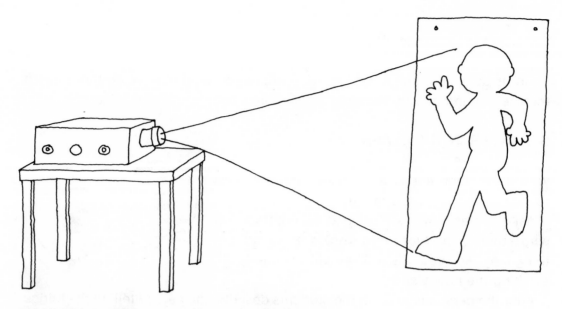

SHADOW SHAPES (no reading required)

(*Objectives*—learning to work together, and observing the physical differences in one another.)

Take a large sheet of brown paper and tack it to the wall. Use a projector for the bright light to make a shadow. Have a friend trace your shape. Show as much movement as you can. Put it on the floor and cut out your shape. Tape your shape up on the wall.

Teaching Suggestions:

- Write a story about yourself and put it up on your shape.
- Make up a game of guessing each other's shapes.
- Discover the differences and similarities in each other's shapes.
- Discuss how God planned to make each person different with different talents.
- Pick a shape and imitate it to music.

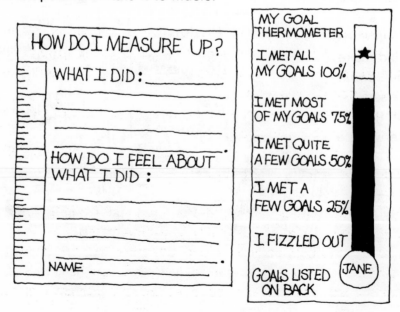

Effective Organizing

The teacher who wishes to individualize instruction has many things to consider. There are not only physical and intellectual differences in students but vast diversities in religious backgrounds and experiences. The teacher may desire to meet these needs but the organizational task seems overwhelming. The following ideas for organizing materials, classrooms, and students may assist you with this task.

. . . organizing materials

Your first problem in organizing materials for your class will be deciding what should be ordered. Let us look at a somewhat typical class group:

John—an ideal student. His parents are active in the church and he has been in Bible school since he was a baby.

Mary—sharp as a whip. She is extremely active and hard to keep occupied because she grasps and finishes everything quickly.

Bill—has been around for a long time. He appears to be gradually losing interest. He is a poor reader and books are a frustration. You are afraid you'll lose him in another year or so.

Ruth—rides the church bus. She knows nothing about the Bible. In fact, she doesn't even own one because her family is not interested.

Tony—in a N.H. (neurologically handicapped) class in public school. He was more often under the chair than on it until last year. Now he is belligerent and loses his temper easily. He can learn but does not stay with any task for long.

Sue—in a public school class for "exceptional" children or slow learners. She is a sweet, gentle child but seems able to do very little. The workbook is too hard and she can't read even the easiest words.

Your class presentation, followed by a discussion and a workbook "follow-up" is definitely not going to meet the individual needs of this highly diverse, yet not unusual, group. You are convinced there must be a better way! There is, but it is not *one way.* To substitute just one different way of instruction will simply replace one problem with another. If you are teaching mainly for students like John, which we often do, then will you change and teach in your new way for Sue? Then what will happen to John? And so the problem multiplies.

Begin by considering the materials you order. Why order the *same* material for children who are *not* the same? Is it really necessary to order exactly the same thing for every child in your class? Consider some alternatives.

Since your students do not all have the same reading abilities, why not order some Primary papers *and* some Middler papers. Order some of one workbook and some of another. Then add a few Bible crossword puzzle books for Mary and John and forget about the workbooks for them altogether.

"Wait a minute! I can't get away with that," you protest. "Students' feelings will be hurt if it says *Beginner* and they are *Primaries.*" Possibly this is true, but not so likely if you take the time to explain your new way of doing things. You are more likely to have concerns by *parents* than from students, so be sure parents, too, understand your goals. *Keep these two things in mind:*

- Bright children really *do not* feel proud of their work when it was too easy to begin with.
- Slower children *do* feel proud when they are able to do the work, even if they have been given different work.

The teacher who strives to stress *accomplishment* for *each* child, rather than comparing one child with another, is well on the road to successful individualizing.

On the following pages are some ideas to help you with your organization and use of multi-level materials.

COLOR CODE MATERIALS

Cut the pages apart from all the assorted levels of story papers and activity papers you can find. Leftover papers are great for this. Mount them on colored paper using a different color for each approximate level of difficulty. But all of one color in a folder and/or box of the same color.

As you enlarge your collection you can separate the items within each box by category. Within each category have a folder for various commonly taught topics—Bible characters, parables, miracles, etc.

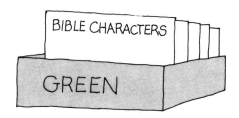

After you tell a story, let the students select a story or activity card from the appropriate box you suggest. Follow up by letting them share their stories with one another.

COLOR CODING MAY BE DONE IN MANY WAYS:

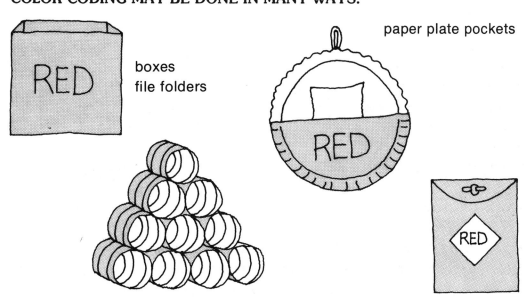

boxes
file folders

paper plate pockets

3 lb. coffee cans mounted on a board
or epoxy glued together in a pyramid

large envelopes with a colored
shape glued on the front

put materials in packets

Use multilevel materials as the basis for making up individual packets for students. Watch the interest soar as each child eagerly opens his own specially prepared packet on Sunday morning.

The "packet" might be:
- an envelope he decorated himself
- a shoe box
- a file folder
- a round cereal box or coffee can

Inside the "packet" might be:
- an appropriate take-home paper
- a Bible puzzle
- a personal Scripture message
- a personal note from the teacher
- a cassette to listen to at home and then return
- an activity to do at home

HERE ARE SOME IDEAS FOR PACKET ACTIVITIES:

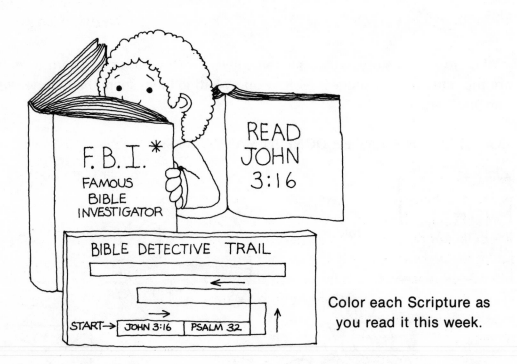

Color each Scripture as you read it this week.

Remember to keep activities for individual packets appropriate to the ability level of the child. Observe carefully each week the kinds of activities your pupils do most successfully and collect similar ideas for their packets. When you see a good idea, write it out and drop it in your own envelope or resource file. Once you start, more and more ideas will come to you.

BIBLE BAG-INS
Ages 3-9

Glue two envelopes to outside of bag. Mark them true and false. Put a set of true-false cards with Bible statements in bag. Student sorts cards into the correct envelope on the outside of bag. (Bible Bag-In)

Prepare bag as shown. Use cards and write a short Bible story, one sentence or part of a sentence on each card. Student removes cards from bag and arranges them in correct order, putting in envelopes. (Bible Story Bag)

Glue three envelopes on bag. Label them people, animals, and plants. Glue small pictures of people, animals, or plant life on cards. Let children sort cards by putting them in the right envelope on the bag. (God's Creations Bag)

BIBLE TEASERS
Ages 3-5
(A good activity for the Noah set)

Using four different colors and four different patterns, cut out four colored shapes and four patterned shapes. Make birds, stars, fish, and Bibles—or select other shapes you like. You will end up with eight of each shape, all different colors and patterns.

Activity:

Younger children match shapes, colors, and/or patterns.

Older children will be challenged (try it—it's hard!) by trying to get a row of four different colors, patterns, and shapes. Put the shapes in a big brown envelope. Be sure to decorate it and put the directions on the outside.

CUT, PASTE, AND LAMINATE

Never, never throw away outdated lesson papers, workbooks (unused or partly used), lesson pictures, or anything unless you have checked it carefully for materials you can use.

EASY PUZZLES
Primary, Beginner

Cut holes in manila envelopes, reinforce holes, and hang them on a hook or pegboard. (Easy to get and put away by preschoolers.)

Cut simple pictures in half. Be sure to cut apart with only two or three large, clear matching sections as shown on envelope. Laminate the pieces. Put only three or four sets in an envelope. Fun for preschoolers and beginners. No reading required.

SPLIT FAMILIES

Ages 8-12

Cut hearts or other shapes from heavy, colored poster board. (Laminate or cover with clear plastic for durability.) Print "pairs" on hearts as shown. Cut apart like puzzle pieces. Include 5-10 pairs, depending on ages of students, in each manila envelope. Put an answer key in a small envelope on front for student self-checking.

Directions:

Match the Bible couples by fitting together the heart puzzles.

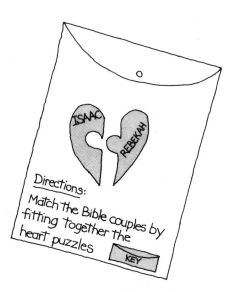

Bible-story paper pictures are colorful and have many uses:

- Cut them out and glue to a large piece of tagboard. Staple several sheets of lined paper under a picture. Children may write their version of the story, make up a story, or write an appropriate Scripture on the paper. After sharing it with the teacher or the class, the paper can be torn off and the next clean paper is ready for someone else.

- Glue large pictures (without too much detail) to heavy cardboard. Cut them apart when thoroughly dry to make your own picture-puzzles. Laminate if possible.
- Let children use pictures to decorate individual "packets."
- File pictures by topic in your own resource box for use with some idea you come up with in the future.
- Cut apart a cartoon version of a short Bible story. Glue the pictures *in the wrong order* to heavy construction paper. Laminate the whole sheet. Let students use a grease pencil to number the pictures in the right order. Give

them a Scripture reference to help if necessary. Rub off the numbers and the activity is ready for someone else!

- Cut short stories out of different level Bible-story papers. Mount them with rubber cement in a tagboard folder. (You will probably need two copies of the paper.) Write a few simple questions on the back of the folder.

An excellent investment for a large Bible school is a laminating press. Many of the activity pages, crossword puzzles, maps, etc., done by students on papers can be laminated and reused many times. If laminating is not possible, acetate folders or envelopes can be secured from stationary supply stores. The worksheets, etc., can be put inside these and the acetate written on with grease pencils. An advantage of the folders or envelopes is that the inside sheets can be changed when desired.

keep materials in a resource center

Many of the teacher-made materials discussed will be stored in your class area. However, many times teachers fail to make efficient use of their time and materials because they are not informed of all their resources. The best way to share is to establish a central media or resource center. In the beginning it may be just a closet or some shelves or a cabinet in the corner of a room. Shelves, a small file cabinet, some large boxes for mounted pictures and maps, and a card file will get you started. A small bulletin board is helpful for posting notices of new materials and a calendar for reserving equipment and materials.

Put all filmstrips, records, tapes, equipment, games, pictures, and transparencies that are not used frequently by a department or a class in the resource center. It is not good stewardship to purchase duplicate materials or equipment, when one item can easily be shared by several classes. Valuable material is, unfortunately, sometimes even forgotten as classes change teachers or departments change leaders.

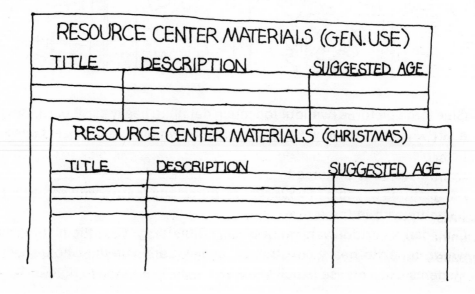

RESOURCE CENTER MATERIALS (GEN. USE)		
TITLE	DESCRIPTION	SUGGESTED AGE

RESOURCE CENTER MATERIALS (CHRISTMAS)		
TITLE	DESCRIPTION	SUGGESTED AGE

A resource center chairman, secretary, or committee should be appointed. Once materials are collected, a complete listing should be prepared and duplicated for every teacher. Pages can be added to the listing as new materials are added, or blank pages can be included in the listing so teachers can write in new items.

It is helpful if materials are followed by a brief description and a suggested appropriate age range. Many listings contain separate pages for seasonal materials.

use bulletin boards for a purpose

An excellent way to provide students with learning opportunities is through the use of bulletin boards.

Many books and pamphlets are available that provide bulletin board ideas. Unfortunately, many of these stress ideas for bulletin boards as decorations. The wise teacher will use this valuable space not only as decoration, but also as a learning experience.

HERE ARE SOME STARTER IDEAS:

Select pictures from your file illustrating good behavior and poor behavior. Put two envelopes on the bulletin board, one containing some round "happy faces" and the other some "sad faces." Let the children tack the faces under the appropriate pictures.

Tack up current lesson pictures and provide memory verses on cards for students to tack under the correct lesson picture.

Laminate or cover large Bible-land maps with heavy plastic. Let students use a grease pencil to trace routes or identify locations. When one child or small group is finished, rub the map off and the activity is ready for someone else.

This activity can be done on a bulletin board or as an individual activity on a smaller piece of poster board. Put a Scripture reference on one card, a memory verse on another. If the child correctly matches, he will see the same symbol when he "flips" up the two cards.

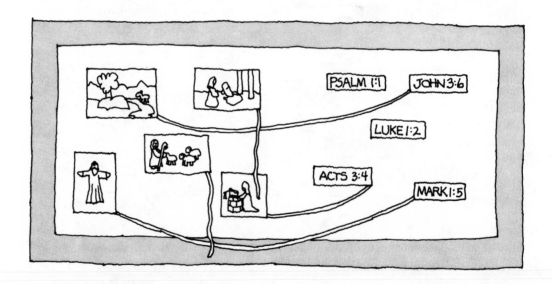

Select several mounted Bible pictures from your collection. On another card, print the appropriate Bible reference for each picture. Tack the pictures and cards on your bulletin board with a long piece of yarn attached below each picture. Let students use the yarn to match the picture with the correct Scripture.

storage ideas:

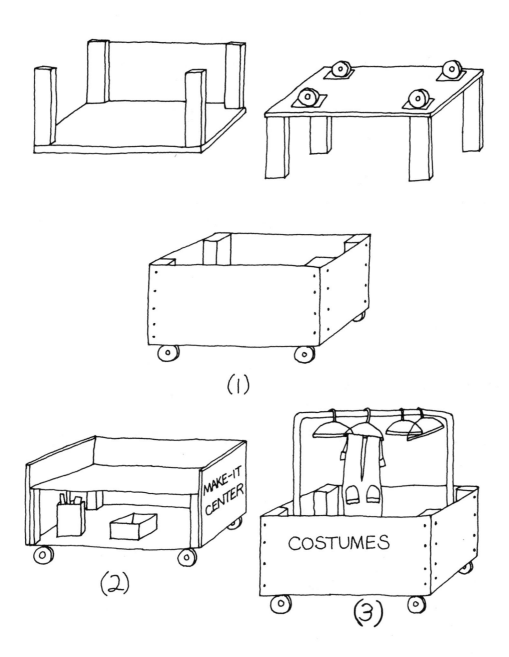

(1)

(2)

MAKE-IT CENTER

COSTUMES

(3)

CONVERTED TABLE FOR STORAGE

Turn an old table upside down. Close in the four sides with plywood. Put casters on the table top. Use it to store scrap materials for activities. (1)

Or, close in three sides about 10″ higher than the length of the legs. Add a shelf across the legs. Add casters. Use as a rolling art center with supplies below and work space on the shelf. (2)

Or, add two posts and a rail to the rolling box. Store costumes for Bible plays in the space below. Hang costumes in use on the rail. (3)

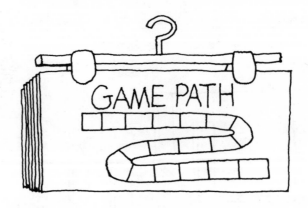

POSTER STORAGE

It is sometimes difficult to find adequate storage for large posters. The posters or charts used at learning centers or for instruction can be saved for future use in this simple way.

Clip as many as eight posters or mounted pictures on a skirt hanger. Hang it in a closet, against the wall, or on the back of a door.

. . . organizing the classroom

Once you have made the decision to move in the direction of individualizing your instruction, you will want to take a critical look at your classroom. Does every part of the room offer the potential for a learning experience? Are books, files, and shelves arranged so they can be used easily by students? Use the following checklist to help determine you classroom needs:

- Is there an area for independent work?
- Are there separated areas for small and large groups?
- Are noisy and quiet areas well defined?
- Are there labels giving directions for each area?
- Are there adequate containers, shelves, and files for activities and materials? Are they available to students?
- Is wall space being used for instruction as well as decoration?
- Is there a place for listening to tapes or records?
- Is there a place for small group or individual viewing of films or filmstrips?

It is not expected that any one classroom would contain all of the ideas on the next few pages. Some of the suggestions may be of help as you consider your own classroom space.

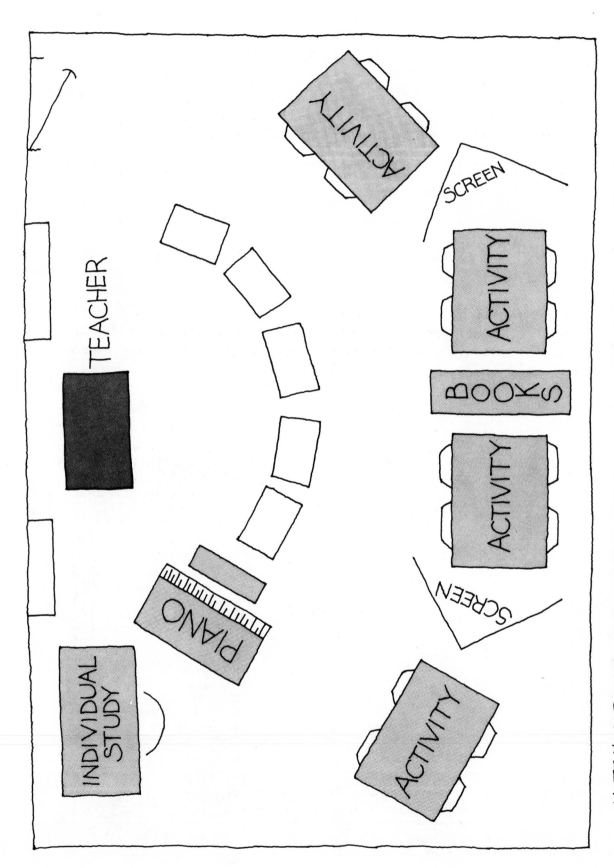

NOTE HOW BOOKS AND SCREENS HELP SHIELD GROUPS, AND PIANO MAKES A PRIVATE CORNER FOR INDIVIDUAL STUDY. IN THIS PLAN THE TEACHER CAN KEEP EYE CONTACT WITH ALL GROUPS.

Individual carrels or booths may be made from simple materials. Grocery boxes fastened together with masking tape can be covered with adhesive-backed paper or wallpaper. Corrugated cardboard can also be shaped into simple booths.

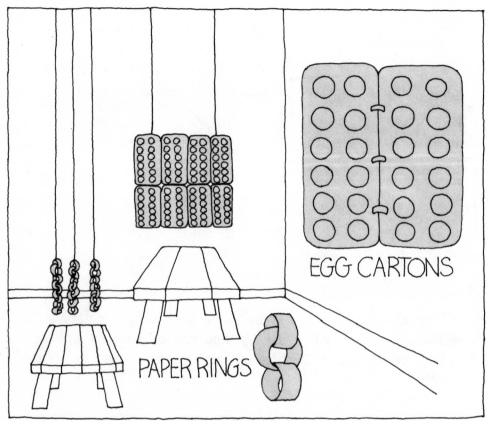

EGG CARTONS

PAPER RINGS

Room dividers are helpful for cutting both sight and sound and for defining activity areas. Bulletin board screens, flannelboards, bookshelves, unused sewing cutting boards, and furniture can be used to screen areas. Try to use both sides for display. Sometimes egg cartons joined together or paper rings are hung from the ceiling to provide simple screens.

BIBLE STUDY

RECORD CASE

CASSETTES

QUIET ZONE
GENIUS AT WORK

A CLOSET DOOR, OPENED PERMANENTLY, CAN CREATE A QUIET CORNER FOR A SMALL GROUP AS WELL AS A PRACTICAL STORAGE

A small table, a sawhorse, or a large box can provide storage for large maps, charts, posters, or children's projects. Turn a sawhorse upside down and place bulky items between the legs.

sawhorse

large box

JESUS OUR LORD

POSTERS AND MAPS

upside-down table

If file drawers are not available, watch for sturdy boxes for filing. Students' papers and workbooks, when filed, can easily be removed and put away by the youngest school-age child. Use colored poster board, cardboard, or heavy paper for dividers. Designs or pictures on the dividers make them easier to identify by younger children. Numbers on the dividers and materials will make the put-away job easy.

Smaller boxes can serve for the teacher's resource files. Such a file is invaluable as a handy reference for the materials and activities in the classroom. It is also a way to record new ideas for use in the future. Resource cards can be categorized for quick referral.

Categories might include:

audiovisual material	field trips	plays
books	games for groups	puzzles
Bible art	games for individuals	seasonal projects
discussions	human resources	stories

Whatever the categories selected by the individual teacher, it is important that the resource file be meaningful and useful.

Boxes, with their covers standing up against them, make fine storage, plus a place for labels or directions. Put picture covers from used greeting cards in one box. New cards can be made by pasting the picture on a single fold of white or colored paper.

Good housekeeping is easy when each item has a place. Children will enjoy putting things away with these simple storage ideas.

Staple cards to cloth shoe-holder pockets to label them for storage. Three by five-inch activity cards will also fit in these pockets.

Use colored paper and cut out shapes of articles placed on an activity table. Masking tape will hold them in place. After items are used, it will be easy to return them to their proper place. This idea works very well for preschoolers.

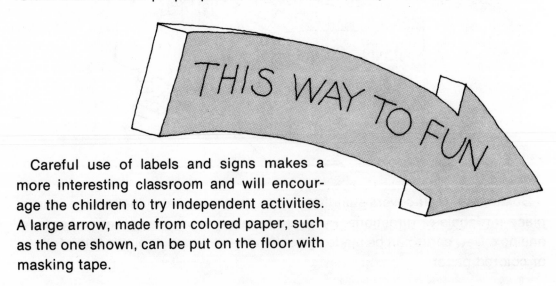

Careful use of labels and signs makes a more interesting classroom and will encourage the children to try independent activities. A large arrow, made from colored paper, such as the one shown, can be put on the floor with masking tape.

Containers that come into our homes can be made into sturdy storage items. Cut-off plastic jugs can be stapled or glued together with epoxy glue. Add a dowel (or better yet, the handle of a broken toy shovel) down the center for a scissors, paintbrush, crayon, or "what-have-you" holder. And don't forget about stacking large cans.

A scrap of plywood, paneling, or pegboard can be used to hold cut-off plastic containers. Use various sizes of plastic liquid soap bottles. Cut them off just below the narrow top. Glue scraps of rickrack or other trim around the top for decoration. Screw the bottles to the backboard. When hung on the wall, this makes a sturdy container for miscellaneous items such as shown in the shoe-bag holder.

... organizing students

Why have small groups? In its purest sense, individualizing should provide every child with learning experiences suited to his or her needs and abilities. First, consider some of the characteristics of a good group learning situation:

Room arrangement. The chairs should be arranged so that seating provides for a face-to-face rather than audience situation. Participants in a group activity need to be able to look at each other.

Intercommunication. There is communication among pupils as well as between teacher and pupils. Students are free to seek assistance from others in the group. The group shares in decision-making rather than having all decisions made by the teacher.

Resolving conflicts. The emphasis is placed upon the group's resolution of conflicts when they occur, rather than the teacher's policing.

Cooperation and leadership role. Pupils share in the leadership role with the teacher, being free to disagree and make proposals. Group rules and goals are accepted by all members of the group, with the group members helping to enforce rules and meet goals.

Evaluation. Deciding whether or not goals have been met becomes a group problem, rather than a teacher opinion.

Teacher role. The role of the teacher becomes that of a member of the group, assisting and guiding, rather than that of director who sets all goals and procedures.

The extent to which these characteristics are found within a group will be determined by the skill of the teacher and the age level and experience of the students. They are, however, worthy goals to keep in mind as we endeavor to recognize the importance of meeting individual needs. As we instruct our entire group, a small group, or individuals, we will want to consider some different techniques.

how to begin

Having gathered some ideas and rearranged the classroom furniture, what comes next? Each teacher will start in a slightly different way, but you are always advised to make changes slowly.

You may wish to begin with one small group, working apart from the balance of the class, for a portion of your class time. To avoid cries of "favoritism," change the group and, if necessary, the activity weekly. Children will be anxious for their turn at the special activity. Discuss behavior rules and other procedures carefully with the class. Plenty of time taken here can avoid problems later.

As groups become accustomed to working apart from the teacher and the class, additional small groups can be added. You will continue, however, to keep some of your time for whole-group activities. A three-week schedule might look like this:

15 minutes—*whole group*
          songs, Scriptures, prayers, etc.
 5 minutes—prepare for groups
          review procedures
          get materials
15 minutes—*3 small groups*
          Red—Bible story with teacher
          Blue—cassette story with questions to answer
          Green—Bible crossword puzzle to do together
 5 minutes—return to whole group
          discuss work
20 minutes—*whole group*
          art work, workbook, story paper,
          cleanup, songs, dismissal

In such a plan, the children remain with the same group for three weeks, each week going to a different activity. While the activities can be left the same for the three weeks, it is easy for the teacher to make a simple adjustment to accommodate the ability of the group. For example, on a particular Sunday, the "Green" table puzzle can be changed to accommodate a more or less capable group.

While it is possible to organize an entire, large department for small group activities, space in which to move usually becomes the critical factor. However, careful timing can often solve space problems.

A few years ago a church wanted to boost interest and improve the program for a department of sixty 4th, 5th, and 6th graders. Their traditional pattern had been:

Bible school 9:30-10:30 A.M.
Junior church at 10:45-11:30 A.M.

A number of problems had arisen. The opening session took too long. Teachers with small groups of grade-level students had only about 20 minutes to teach the lesson. Many students were leaving at 10:30, so it was difficult to extend the teaching period to 10:45. The Junior church time became too lengthy for the younger children, especially when it had to be extended to correspond to an "overtime" church service.

To solve these problems, the staff decided to plan a thirty-minute interim session between the Bible school and Junior church, moving to a nearby fellowship hall after the adult class had left for church. The total time period now looked like this:

Bible-school opening	9:30-9:55
Bible-school lesson with teacher	10:00-10:35
organize groups and move to new area	10:35-10:45
small group sessions	10:45-11:15
Junior church	11:20-11:45

For the new group activity sessions, the students were organized into six groups of ten children. The sequence of six learning activities took two weeks to complete, with each given group doing three short activities each Sunday. The first two or three Sundays the children referred to the following chart, but after they became familiar with the plan, they seldom looked at it.

group	Sunday 1 activity number			Sunday 2 activity number		
A	1	2	3	4	5	6
B	2	3	1	5	6	4
C	3	1	2	6	4	5
D	4	5	6	1	2	3
E	5	6	4	2	3	1
F	6	4	5	3	1	2

The numbered activities were varied to suit the lesson activities and materials available. A sample of the activities for one two-week series follows:

Activity 1—Listening to a teacher-prepared story on the tape recorder with the children using headsets. (Listening posts, using multiple outlet boxes, can be purchased and will plug into record players, tape recorders, or combination filmstrip-record player outfits.)

Activity 2—A discussion group with an adult leader.

Activity 3—A puzzle, quiz, or game with a student group leader in charge.

Activity 4—A filmstrip with record. Student operated. The filmstrip was followed by questions to answer orally with a student leader.

Activity 5—A discussion group with an adult leader.

Activity 6—A game, puzzle, or quiz with a group leader in charge. You will notice that each week one of the three activities was meeting with an adult leader. These adults were not always department teachers. Other resource people from the church were used, depending on the topic being studied.

The activities were planned for short spans of time. Discipline problems were at a minimum because students had to keep busy in order to finish.

Students and teachers must be thoroughly prepared for this type of work. Be sure to consider these things:

1. Selection of groups and group leaders.

2. Instruction for group leader on use of equipment.

3. Discussions of consideration for others both in your group and in other groups. Rewind tapes, straighten chairs, etc., leaving area ready for the next group.

4. Group leaders may delegate responsibility, but equipment may be operated only by those who have had instruction.

ADVANTAGES? Here are a few of the evident ones:

1. The students develop responsibility and independence as they learn for themselves.

2. Leadership is improved as students learn to be responsible for materials and equipment, relying very little on adult assistance.

3. Students have the opportunity to discuss lessons informally by themselves and also with an adult leader.

4. Restlessness and lack of interest are practically nil because each group activity is short and to the point. Frequent movement keeps students eager to find out "What's coming next?"

5. Students become *active* learners, *participating* rather than listening to a teacher for long time periods.

6. The boys and girls thought it was great and could hardly wait for this "small group" portion of the morning to arrive. Instead of students leaving, they were insisting that their parents *stay* for church so they could remain also.

PROBLEMS? Most can be avoided, if you will apply the following:

1. Plan each series of lessons carefully. If you have older students, include them in your planning. Poor planning will bring about disappointing results in any program.

2. Make sure all equipment works. Make quick, last-minute checks on Sunday morning. Faulty equipment can really ruin your time schedule. Assign this responsibility to one of the department teachers.

3. Select all stories, puzzles, games, and discussion topics with the greatest of care. Make sure they suit your age group and the lesson goals. Make sure you *preview* filmstrips and records (and tapes, if you do not prepare them yourselves) to be certain they are appropriate. Materials selected by titles and advertising reviews can be quite different from the way they are described.

4. Don't be concerned if you must make changes. Be ready constantly to evaluate. Realize that in any innovative program you must expect to make continual improvements.

Colors are a quick and easy way to identify groups for any age level. Colored slips of paper or adhesive-backed colored disks stuck to name tags can be given to students on arrival. Group meeting areas can be identified by a large sheet of colored paper on a table. Teachers who routinely use grouping may want to make a more permanent way for displaying colors or group labels:

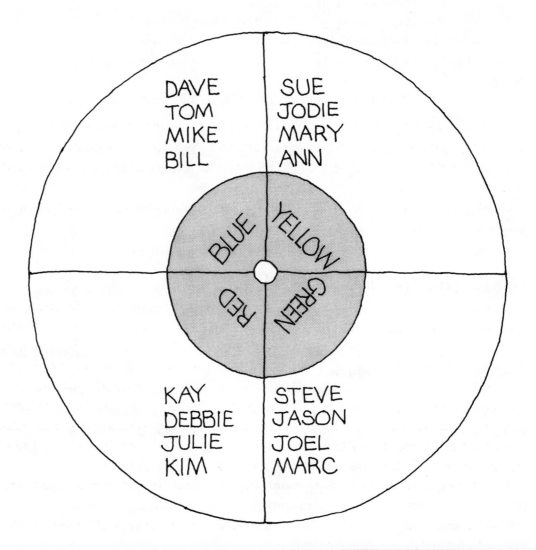

An easy way to organize for several groups is shown. Make a large white disk for the background. Make a smaller white disk for the center. Then cut four colors to glue on it, as shown. Make a hole in the center of both disks and fasten them together with a paper fastener so the top disk will turn. Put the names of your groups on the large disk. Students whose names appear with the red section will go to that center for their activity. Short group activities can be changed more than once in a class period, or changed weekly, if there is only one group meeting in a week. If you cover the large disk with heavy clear plastic, or laminate it, you can write the names on the plastic with a grease pencil and then rub them off when you wish to change groups.

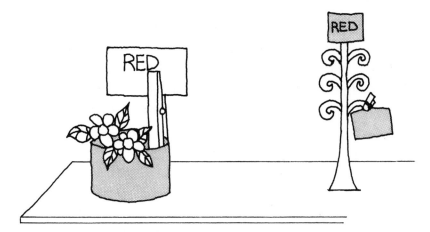

Spray can tops filled with plaster of paris and a clothespin and plastic flower make fine holders. These can be used for color identification (the flower), and instructions can be placed on a card in the clothespin. If desired, a colored card can be put in the clothespin.

Cup holders can be used in a similar way, with a colored card in the top and individual or group instructions clipped to each holder.

whole group individualizing

Individualizing while instructing your entire class can be tricky. Be careful in the way you phrase questions. Avoid questions with predetermined right answers. The children will be busy searching for *your* right answer rather than voicing their opinions. And, if you get silly, thoughtless answers, ask more questions to help the student clarify his or her thinking: "What do you mean?" "Can you explain to us more?" "Why do you think that?" The "pop-off" student who is treated seriously and asked to explain a response will soon come up with more thoughtful contributions. If scolded or ridiculed, he or she will continue along the same line, having received the expected response.

Suggestions for whole group activities that allow for individual responses are:

Open-ended stories. Read a character-building story to your class but let the students write or tell their own endings.

Questions for individual responses. Older children may write answers.

Younger students might tell teachers their ideas to be recorded on chart paper or the blackboard.

—If you received $10, how would you use it?

—If you could relive any one day, which day would it be?

—If you were a leader in our church, what changes would you try to make?

—If you could be someone else, who? Why?

Teach new routines. Explain new games and practice them together. These can later be used as small group activities. Explain the rules for use of a new learning situation.

Teach use of equipment. Teach the students how to properly use and care for equipment. A filmstrip projector, cassette tape player, and record player can be handled by Primary children if they are properly taught its use.

Special programs and guest speakers. You may want to build up a file of special "human resources" from the membership of your church. Short special programs and talks can greatly motivate and interest your students.

small groups

Keep in mind that any number over five decreases the effectiveness of a discussion group. Otherwise, your small group number should be limited to the requirement for the particular activity, ideally no more than ten students.

It is necessary to establish routine procedures for small group work. These might be made into a chart:

Some teachers find it helpful to designate a group leader for the day, or for a longer period of time, who is responsible for checking to see that routine procedures are followed. The leader can also be the person to handle equipment, thus saving some confusion or argument among the group members.

After beginning by assigning groups to activities, the teacher may wish to try some other types of scheduling. Here are some suggestions:

Choice of activities. The teacher assigns a group to a particular activity area, but once there, each child may select from a number of activities. These may be stories with questions, picture puzzles, games, etc.

Choice of time. Children are assigned to certain learning activities, according to their needs, but they may decide *when* to go to the assigned area.

Contracting. Students, working with the teacher, make an agreement which sets a goal for what they will do and when it will be done.

"God Gave You Ears" is a sample of an enjoyable group activity for young children.

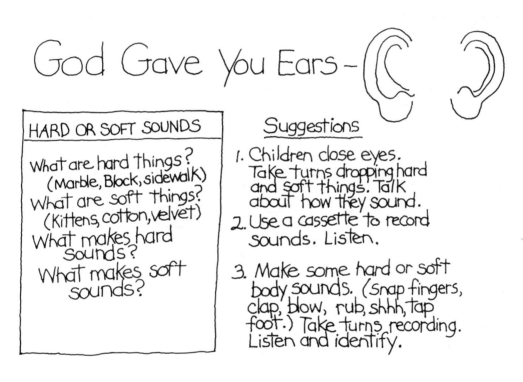

God Gave You Ears —

HARD OR SOFT SOUNDS

What are hard things?
 (Marble, Block, sidewalk)
What are soft things?
 (Kittens, cotton, velvet)
What makes hard
 sounds?
What makes soft
 sounds?

Suggestions

1. Children close eyes. Take turns dropping hard and soft things. Talk about how they sound.
2. Use a cassette to record sounds. Listen.
3. Make some hard or soft body sounds. (Snap fingers, clap, blow, rub, shhh, tap foot.) Take turns recording. Listen and identify.

individual activities

The purpose of individual activities should never be simply to isolate problem children. Few problem children can handle the decision making or self-control needed to carry through an independent activity. They need assistance and support from the teacher or a group.

Well-planned individual activities can be a real asset to your class program, however. They will help children to solve problems and think critically as they learn to rely on their own knowledge. You can begin with easy programmed-style materials made to correlate with your lesson goals.

BIBLE BOOKMARKS
Ages 8-12

Cut out 8 to 10 Bibles from red construction paper. Glue edges of each on larger sheet of black poster board or tack to bulletin board. Leave top of each Bible open so bookmark can be inserted.

Print Bible reference on each Bible, and Scripture on bookmarks. Match by inserting bookmarks in Bibles. Number each bookmark so a key can be made for self-checking.

Move from these to independent activities which lead to more challenging and creative thinking. Many of these activities can be continued at home through the week.

Number questions for an independent study project on a roll-down window shade. Start at the bottom and number to the top.

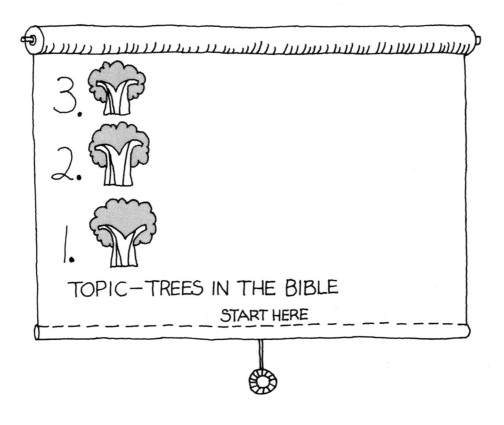

SANDPAPER* BIBLE ALPHABET BOOK

Ages 4-6

*(The more senses used in learning, the greater the likelihood of retention.)

Cut large letters from sandpaper. Glue on heavy construction paper or light-weight poster board about 9″ x 12″. Punch, then reinforce holes. Add a blank white sheet between each letter.

As new Bible lessons are learned, use the appropriate letter to make an alphabet sentence. Let children feel the letter. Feeling will increase memory of the letter and its related lesson.

If possible, laminate your chart on lightweight cardboard. Push paper fasteners through as shown. Stretch a rubber band or use yarn loops and match the pairs.

NO READING
REQUIRED

ALL GOD'S CHILDREN . . .

Go to Bible School!

This can be a small group or individual activity at a bulletin board learning center, or a class activity for attendance. Cut out paper shapes for boys and girls. Younger children may place the correct number of boys and girls on the path to the church. Beginners will enjoy matching the numbers on the figures with the numbers on the path. No reading required.

BIBLE WORD SPIN

Ages 6-9

Every teacher is a reading teacher. No subject, skill, or knowledge can be isolated from reading. Reading skills are basic to all understanding.

Reading Bible Words:

Use a "pizza" cardboard disk or cut a 12″ or 15″ disk of poster board. Put a beginning consonant on a smaller disk in the center. Write the word endings on the outer disk. The student turns the center to match the endings and tries to say each word. A good partner activity.

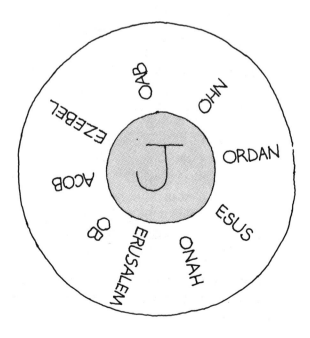

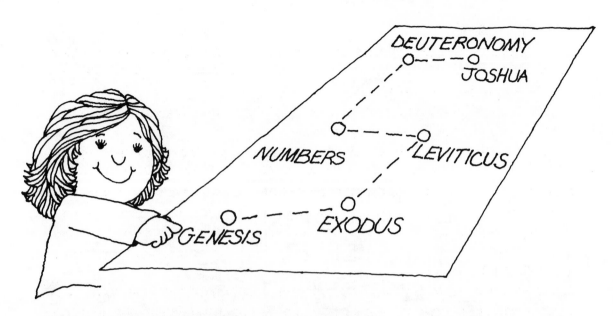

BOOKS OF THE BIBLE DOT-TO-DOT PICTURE

Start with a simple outline picture, printing the names of the books of the Bible at various points, in such a sequence that lines drawn between them would complete the picture. Insert the picture, with carbon paper and blank paper (or a ditto master) in a typewriter. Type over the Bible book names, add dots, but omit all lines. When this is duplicated, you have a dot-to-dot picture using the names of the books of the Bible.

BIBLE BILL
Ages 6-8

Attach head, arms, and cut paper "clothing" to a shoe box. Cut slit or hole in top as shown for belt buckle. Put Bible Bill on a table with pencil and paper, and a Bible for reference. Children write their favorite Scriptures and give them to Bill. Weekly, or as desired, open box and read Bill's messages.

MINI-CENTER

A mini-center gives lots more students a chance to participate. The important thing is to keep the time limit low—three to five minutes. Use a three minute egg timer if you like—or try this:

Put a bowl of small, wrapped hard candy at the center. The student may stay at the center only until his candy is gone!

This involves a lot of *teacher trust,* but most children are surprisingly honest.

The matching activity below is a good one for a mini-center. Although it uses rubber bands (sometimes a problem with children who are too imaginative!), it works well at the mini-center. Children are so busy trying to beat the time limit they don't have time to think up extra activities for the rubber bands!

MATCHING ACTIVITY

Use a piece of scrap lumber. Pound in, evenly spaced, eight or ten small nails on each side. Line up matching lists on outside of nails and tack them in place. (Lists are not permanent, so can be changed from time to time to suit your lessons or student needs.) Supply eight or ten appropriately-sized rubber bands for matching.

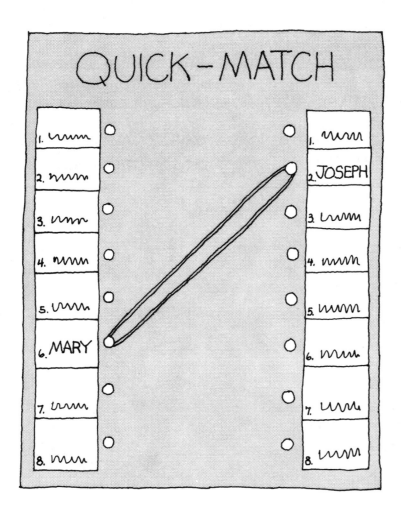

WHICH IS WHICH?

Ages 9-13

Prepare a bulletin board as shown. Glue on it, or tack up, two large brown envelopes.

Cards to be sorted may be books of the Bible, people clearly identified with Old or New Testament, or outstanding Bible events.

List the answers in two lists on the key for self-checking.

OLD TESTAMENT OR NEW TESTAMENT?

Put a slit on each half of a shoe box lid. Cover with contact paper, wallpaper, or other attractive material. Draw a line down the middle of the lid and print *New Testament* on one side and *Old Testament* on the other.

Put a cardboard divider in the center of the inside of the shoe box. On small cards write names of Bible people, events, or Scripture references. Students decide which Testament the card fits and put it in the correct slit.

Glue an envelope to one end of the box and put the correct listing for each Testament so students can correct their own work. Add new cards as you study new events and people.

BIBLE STORY COMIC STRIP

Cut apart the strips (or if easy and short, single pictures) from a Bible story comic strip. Laminate the strips or pictures. Put them in an envelope appropriately decorated. Children can remove the pieces and arrange them in the right sequence.

STARTERS FOR MATCHING GAMES

These are starters to get you going for matching games. Add to your list by asking your students to help you. Provide blank cards and an envelope or box for them and you'll be amazed at how many you can collect!

GO TOGETHER PEOPLE

Samson	— Delilah
David	— Jonathan
Cain	— Abel
Mary	— Joseph
Moses	— Aaron
Abraham	— Sarah
Hagar	— Ishmael
Jacob	— Esau
Adam	— Eve
Priscilla	— Aquila
Ruth	— Boaz
Isaac	— Rebekah

GO TOGETHER PEOPLE AND PLACES

Noah	— Mt. Ararat
Moses	— Mt. Sinai
Solomon	— Jerusalem
Jonah	— Nineveh
Lot	— Sodom & Gomorrah
Abraham	— The Promised Land
Joshua	— Jericho
Jesus	— Nazareth
Jacob	— Bethel
Elijah	— Mt. Carmel
Lazarus	— Bethany
Nebuchadnezzar	— Babylon

FOAM RUBBER SQUARES

Foam rubber blocks are great—they make no noise when thrown—try 'em, you'll like 'em!

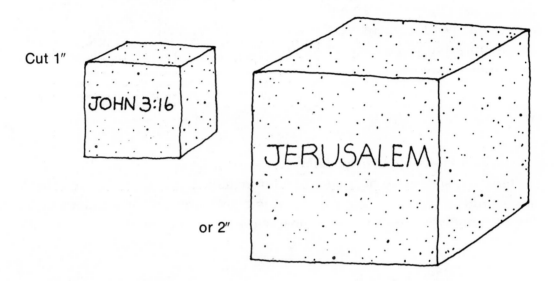

Cut 1″

JOHN 3:16

or 2″

JERUSALEM

squares of foam rubber. Use a felt-tip marker to write on sides. Uses:

1. *For Scripture memory:*
   If a student can say the Scripture he throws, he gets a point.
2. *To learn Bible words:*
   If a student can say the word he throws, he gets a point.
3. Any time you need "dice" to throw for a game.

SCHEDULING IDEAS FOR THE BULLETIN BOARD

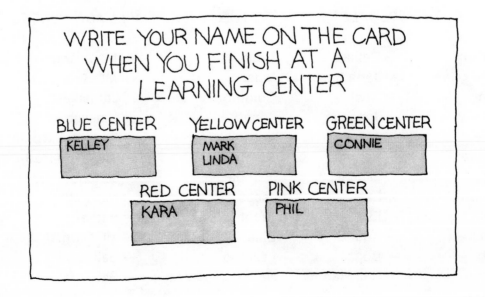

WRITE YOUR NAME ON THE CARD
WHEN YOU FINISH AT A
LEARNING CENTER

BLUE CENTER
KELLEY

YELLOW CENTER
MARK
LINDA

GREEN CENTER
CONNIE

RED CENTER
KARA

PINK CENTER
PHIL

7

Effective Evaluating

Rid yourself of the idea that evaluation is simply, and often sadly, a letter grade, or a poor, fair, good, or excellent rating of an individual. These systems take little consideration of our Scriptural advice to consider each person according to the gifts God has given him or her (Romans 12:6). They are seldom a true evaluation of learning. They are, instead, a comparison of one child to another, the very thing to avoid in treating students as individuals. God has told us that each one has his or her own unique gift. It is up to us, as teachers, to help students find that gift and develop it.

Effective evaluation should motivate. One way to help students develop is to encourage them to work. Reward for a job well done makes students want to try to do good work. Praise is one form of reward. When a group of teachers was asked to make a list of motivating rewards that encouraged students to work and do a good job, they had these suggestions:

choice of work	draw on the board
choice of game	lunch with the teacher
library time	verbal praise
special jobs	choose a song
get a star	read to the teacher
get candy or gum	select story for teacher to read aloud
move chair or desk	tape a story on a cassette
get a certificate	get a bookmark
be a leader	"goof-off" time allowed
do art work	visit another class

What about the child who doesn't earn much praise or win many rewards? Unless you are careful, you will be giving that child negative feedback: "Don't do that," "Sit down," and "Sit still." Remember to praise children for *low level* work, or even mildly acceptable behavior if you expect them to move to a higher level. Some children may have to be rewarded for just doing *something* at first, even though the work is not complete. Others, with behavior problems, must be praised for doing *nothing,* odd as it may sound! Forty-nine ways to say, "You can do better," without being overly negative or critical, have been suggested in the September, 1973, issue of *Teacher Magazine* by MacMillan Professional Magazines, Inc. You may wish to try some of these with children who often fail to meet their goals and your expectations:

- "Wouldn't it be better done this way?"
- "That's not too cool."
- "You sure bombed out on this one!"
- "This isn't up to your usual style."
- "Would you like to discuss this?"
- "You must have done this in a hurry."
- "Don't give up."
- "Keep trying, you'll get it yet."
- "Keep working, you've almost got it."
- "I'm glad you're trying."
- "Apparently I didn't explain carefully what you were to do."
- "Keep trying; let me know if I can give you extra help."
- "I know it's difficult, but you can do it."
- "This was a tough day, huh?"
- "Maybe you did this too fast."
- "Does this work satisfy you?"
- "Didn't you like doing this lesson?"
- "Have you suggestions as to how I could make this a more interesting lesson?"

These are just a few of the ways a teacher can *evaluate* but still encourage students to do better work. Remember, your estimation of the work of a student must be in keeping with his or her individual "gifts," not how he or she compares with someone whose gifts are different. Constantly ask yourself, "Is this student doing her best? Is he learning at *his own* rate?"

. . . evaluate for parents

Evaluation for parents can exist for the Bible school. Most parents are interested in their children's religious progress or the children would not be in your class. Again, your evaluation should be based on what projects and activities the child has completed rather than a comparison of one child to another. It should also include an opportunity for parents to participate in self-evaluation in regard to their role in their child's religious progress. You might suggest that parents fill out a self-inventory (not to be returned to you). *Example:*

	YES	NO
Am I reading Bible stories to my child?	_____	_____
Do we have daily family devotions?	_____	_____
Do we read the Bible together daily?	_____	_____
Do we read and follow the home suggestions given to us by our child's teacher?	_____	_____

Evaluation is a two-way street and communication with parents must be an important part of your pupils' religious growth. Many churches plan a formal visit by the teacher to each child's home as part of the yearly instructional program. Some have had Saturday conferences, with parents invited to come to the church and confer with the teacher in the classroom setting. Either of these ideas should be supplemented with many informal communications. Here is one *example:*

THEME: Bibles

ACTIVITY: Today we discussed Bibles. We looked at several different versions of the Bible. (*King James, Living Bible, New International,* etc.) We saw Bibles with both Testaments, and some New Testaments only.

RESULT: As a result of today's lesson your child should be able to tell you the two parts of the Bible and name two or three different Bible versions. You might like to follow up at home by looking at your family Bibles together and discussing them.

_____Teacher

A message such as this to the parents gives them a chance to make *their own* evaluations of what their child is learning, as well as giving them an opportunity to extend the religious experience in the home.

. . . evaluate with students

As Christian teachers interested in each individual, we should consider the most important aspect of evaluation the goal setting we do with our students. This should be done jointly, with pupils and teachers working together. It should continue as long as the person is a student—yes, even into the adult years! This work with younger students should eventually lead the students to personal goal setting and evaluation of their own work. Adults who become lifelong learners are goal-oriented, even though it may no longer be a teacher-pupil experience, or even a conscious action on the part of the adult learner.

Some *examples* of adult goals are:
- "I will get up 10 minutes early every day and read my Bible."
- "I will attend church and Bible school every Sunday."
- "I will read a chapter a day in the Bible."
- "I will have personal devotions every evening."

Adults who learn, set goals! Children need help in learning how to set goals. Further, they must learn how to set *reasonable goals* for themselves as individuals. Goals and evaluation must go hand in hand. If you have no goals, you cannot measure your progress. You will find ideas at the end of the chapter on discipline for individual goal setting. Following are some additional suggestions for goal setting that can be started one week with students and concluded later with self-evaluation. The time period will vary with your projects, plans, and the needs of the individual student.

GOAL SETTING AND COMPETITION

Competition does not need to mean comparison of one child with another. If we are measuring according to the goals set for *individual children,* competition is based on *progress,* not on comparisons of ability. Progress in class or department competition is for *goals met. Example:*

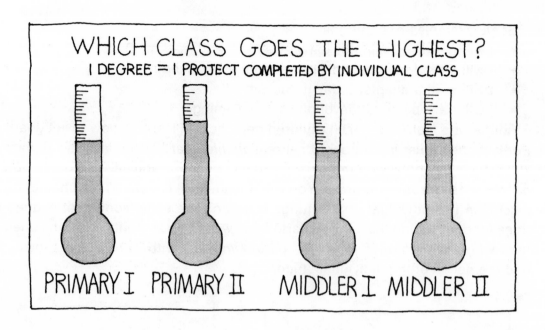

Sometimes it is helpful to send home a report about the day's accomplishments. In this case, set goals at the beginning of the class period and send the form home the same day. Children will complete the form before leaving class. *Example:* (Child puts his name under the appropriate face.)

DEAR _____

LOOK AT ME !

TODAY I WAS :

_____ A GOOD WORKER   _____ A POOR WORKER

_____ A NEAT WORKER   _____ A MESSY WORKER

_____ A QUIET WORKER   _____ A NOISY WORKER

I MADE GOOD PROGRESS – I DID : _____

I MADE POOR PROGRESS – I DID : _____

MYSELF

Some teachers successfully set goals with students for activities to be completed at home. The student takes the record home with him and brings it back completed.

Let the child name his "circle" face (that handy adhesive circle again). He cuts out strips that apply to make his body. If you wish to save gluing, use adhesive-backed file folder labels. For younger children, you will need to fill in the words. For older ones, give them suggested listings and let them fill in their own. *Example:*

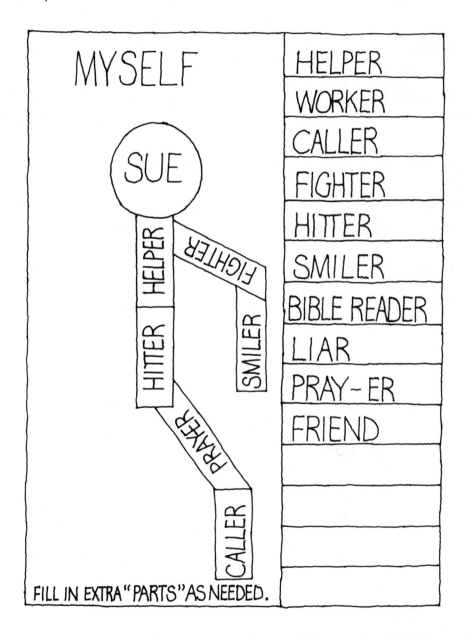

Children may be asked to complete the evaluation form at church, judging their progress on goals set for the past week. Goals may be needed for problem areas in a class. You may wish to adapt these ideas to your own needs:

MY CHECK-UP THIS WEEK

____ DID SOMETHING FOR SOMEONE
____ READ MY BIBLE DAILY
____ LEARNED A BIBLE VERSE
____ INVITED A FRIEND TO BIBLE SCHOOL
____ PHONED SOMEONE IN MY CLASS
         WHO WAS ABSENT (WHO?_____)
         SIGNED _____

ME _____
       NAME

I AM :   YES   NO
IN BIBLE SCHOOL ON TIME   ____   ____
A GOOD WORKER   ____   ____
A HELPER   ____   ____

REWARD STICKERS

Use one-inch colored gummed stickers for balloons for each project completed. Take home when the lesson period of time is over. You can use this idea for stars in the sky, animals in the field, flowers on stems, etc. However, make sure the sticker is for *goals or projects completed,* not just attendance.

KEY RING

Children of all ages seem to enjoy keeping track of goals completed with keys. Make a supply of light cardboard keys. Punch holes and reinforce them. As each child completes a goal, project, or learning center activity, let him take a key and write the name of the project on the key. Tie keys on a piece of heavy yarn and hang them on pegboard hooks or on a bulletin board. Make a colored key with each child's name. Send the "key ring" home at the end of the stated period of time.

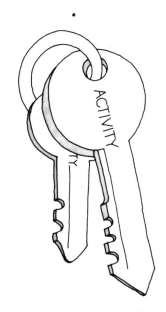

Now, you are brave enough to ask. Sometimes it takes real courage for a teacher to ask students for opinions about their class. However, it is often the best and easiest way to learn whether or not you are meeting the individual needs of your students. Here is a sample of a simple student attitude survey which can be used for children as young as Primary level, if you read the questions to them.

STUDENT ATTITUDE SURVEY

Directions: For each of the four questions below place an "X" in front of the one statement that *best* describes your own attitude.

1. My general opinion of my class:
   ___a. I *like* it *very much.*
   ___b. I *like* it.
   ___c. I can "take it or leave it."
   ___d. I don't particularly like it.
   ___e. I *dislike* it very much.

2. My opinion of my own ability:
   ___a. I am *better* than *most students.*
   ___b. I am *above* average.
   ___c. I am *about* average.
   ___d. I am *below* average.
   ___e. *Most* students are *better* than I.

3. My opinion of my success:

    ___a. I succeed *nearly all* of the time.

    ___b. I succeed *most* of the time.

    ___c. I succeed *some* of the time.

    ___d. I *seldom* succeed.

    ___e. I *almost never* succeed.

4. My opinion of the teacher who teaches me:

    ___a. *Very interested* in me.

    ___b. *Interested* in me.

    ___c. Pays *some attention* to me.

    ___d. Only *slightly interested* in me.

    ___e. *Not interested* in me.

. . . evaluate yourself

In conclusion, there are three vital people in evaluation—the parent, the pupil, and last and most important—the teacher. No, not the teacher as an evaluator of *others,* but as a constant evaluator of *self.* Take the time now to fill out the following self-evaluation. You may find areas where you are already doing an excellent job. Hopefully, you will find some thoughts about where you can improve. You will learn something new about yourself!

God gave you a special gift—your gift is teaching. "For as we have many members in one body, and all members have not the same office . . . having then gifts differing according to the grace that is given to us . . . let us wait on our teaching (Romans 12:4-7 paraphrased).

It is hoped that this book will help you "wait on your teaching."

BIBLE-SCHOOL TEACHER'S SELF-EVALUATION

	Excellent	Good	Poor
I. RECORD KEEPING			
(a) Keeping my own records orderly?			
(b) Keeping complete records for each child?			
(c) Turning in reports, etc., on time?			
II. PLANNING			
(a) Lesson plans meeting individual needs?			
for average students?			
for below average students?			
for above average students?			
(b) Use of clear performance objectives?			
(c) Pre-testing to determine areas of need?			

(d) Objectives posted on chart or board so students know what is expected of them?

(e) Lessons planned in keeping with objectives?

(f) Testing based on objectives taught?

(g) Enrichment activities for those who already know objectives?

(h) Remedial activities for those who are not ready for objectives?

(i) Planning ahead for necessary materials and equipment?

III. INSTRUCTIONAL TECHNIQUES

(a) Am I using a variety of techniques?

    individual activities?

    small group activities?

    instructional games?

    planned oral activities?

    planned listening lessons?

    variety of discussion techniques?

    use of role playing, drama?

IV. USE OF AUDIO AND VISUAL MEDIA

(a) Instruction bulletin boards?

(b) Variety of pictures, maps, charts?

(c) Use of overhead projector?

(d) Use of opaque projector?

(e) Use of filmstrips?

    for large groups?

    for small groups?

    for individual instruction?

(f) Use of tape recorders?

    for large groups?

    for small groups/listening posts?

    for individual instruction?

(g) Use of record players?

    for large groups?

    for small groups/listening posts?

    for individual instruction?

(h) Classroom displays?

(i) Teacher or student created learning centers?

V. CLASSROOM MANAGEMENT

(a) Guiding students to greater independence?

    learning to use new media and materials unassisted at learning centers?

    learning to plan own activities to meet objectives?

    learning to be responsible for own work and materials?

    learning goal setting and self-evaluation procedures?

learning to be flexible in seating arrangements to accommodate grouping and individual activities?

  (b) Meaningful class discussions?

  better understanding of self?

  better understanding of others?

  better understanding of learning objectives?

  (c) Techniques to reinforce desirable behavior?

  warm fuzzies?

  letter to parents?

  bulletin board recognition?

  student of the week?

VI. PERSONAL GROWTH

  (a) Continuing education through reading, Bible-study classes, conventions, Christian seminars, workshops?

  (b) Taking advantage of opportunities to observe other teachers?

  (c) Serving on committees to study new materials, methods, and programs?

  (d) Regular attendance at department meetings?

  (e) Requesting assistance when needed from: department chairman, minister, or expert teacher?

VII. EVALUATION

  (a) Do I and my students communicate with parents about goals and progress?

  (b) Do I make an effort to praise students and let parents know of praiseworthy activities?

  (c) Do I suggest ways for parents to evaluate home religious instruction?

  (d) Do I continually evaluate my own planning and lessons?

▶ *food for thought*

To discriminate is to see how things are different. Can you discriminate between good teaching and poor teaching?